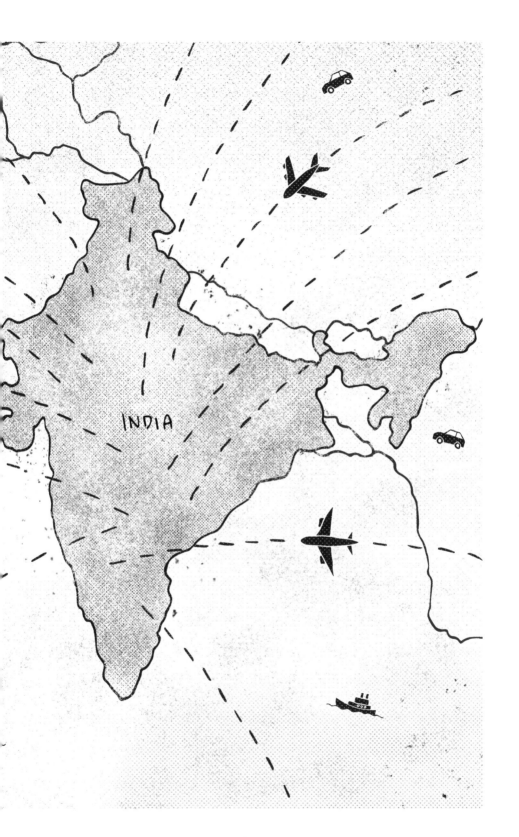

Published by Live Dead Publishing

1445 N. Boonville Ave, Springfield, Missouri 65802

Cover design, typesetting, and interior design by
Prixel Creative (www.prixelcreative.com)

Scripture quotations used in this book taken from
The Message. Copyright © 1993, 1994, 1995, 1996, 2000, 2001, 2002.
Used by permission of NavPress Publishing Group.
Used by permission. All rights reserved.

Names of people in this book have been changed to protect their identities.

ISBN: 978-0-9981789-3-6

Printed in the United States of America

LIVE | DEAD I N D I A

THE COMMON TABLE

INVITING STRANGERS TO BECOME FAMILY

GRATEFUL...

To my common table companions

Who shared their stories:
Born of your very lives, they ring true.

Who dreamed, wrote, and edited alongside me:
John of the mountains, Jackie of the deserts, and Charity of Fort
Worth.

Who saw with spiritual eyes and designed with heart:
Justin, Kendra, and Josiah

And to all who join us around the table

WEST MEETS EAST

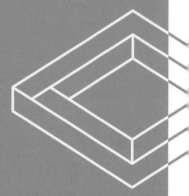

Some naysayers just kicked me in the gut. I need to get out for a few hours to think. I decide to go to a specific hotel that requires the longest drive from where I'm staying. I take my Bible and journal. My heart is in turmoil, and I need to hear something from Jesus.

Questions ring in my head as I drive: What were we thinking attempting to train young Americans and Indians to reach India, the most unreached nation in the world? Is it even possible to blend nationalities and generations together on teams? Is it even possible to take on the staggering number of unreached people groups from diverse religious backgrounds and in settings that range from remote villages to megacities?

I pull into the hotel driveway to very high security and huge vinyl signs advertising a national sports team. I walk into the middle of cricket headquarters: groupies, fans, stalkers, journalists, photographers, coaches and players. I hoped to find a quiet corner, but wouldn't you know it? The hotel is central station for the Rajasthani Royals cricket team. Tomorrow is the big match with Hyderabad, and the place is crazy!

I find a table to sit, order a salad, turn my back to the crowd, open my journal, and start to write.

Inadvertently, I tune into a nearby conversation and recognize an accent. I hear an Australian cricket coach. He is wearing a Hyderabad Devils jersey and eating fish and chips. Multiple dishes of Indian curry and rice are delivered to the table and served onto the plates of three well-dressed Indian gentlemen who must be important. They're educated and articulate, and feel extremely free to express their opinions on the team, the players, and the coach's decisions. The group is discussing strategy for tomorrow's match and the coach's choice to start a certain player. They say he hasn't been scoring well. The Aussie says, "Well, we're not just about that. We're about building a team for the future. If we give these young ones some experience under pressure this year, they'll be ready to win next year."

I think the Holy Spirit just spoke to me!

The coach continues to talk about working with these multi-national young players who live their skills, or lack of them, before hundreds of thousands of adoring fans, playing the most iconic sport in the country of India. "If we can create an environment where the youngsters come onto a level playing field, if we can help them to not compete with each other, they'll actually teach each other. They all come to us with very different and very specific abilities. They can learn from each other. Their biggest drawback is ego."

I scribble as he speaks. I can hardly believe what I'm hearing. I guess if angels, prophets, and donkeys can speak kingdom truths, so can Aussie coaches in coffee shops. And I'm suddenly thinking, "We really are on the right course accepting this diverse group of people. We're doing the right thing in training new teams."

The possibilities to impact India for the fame of Jesus is within reach. The dream of common people from a variety of nations gathering around a common table, inviting strangers who become friends to join us as we live generously sharing the good news, that dream is alive and well in Live Dead India.

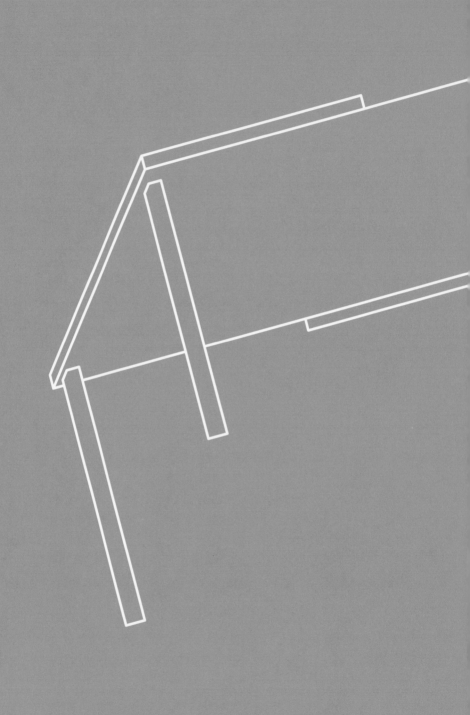

THE GOSPEL DOESN'T NEED A PULPIT.
THE GOSPEL NEEDS A TABLE.

LOSS IS GAIN

None of us knew that we would never again be together like this.

I'm sure we could be heard miles away. We were a raucous crowd gathered around a common table on a roof top in Shantiniketan—an intense, gifted Canadian guy of Indian descent; a lovely, funny social worker from Baltimore; a good-looking, talented Boston musician; a willowy Indian model soon to be married to a man from Dubai; a brilliant Californian of Chinese descent who was a year away from starting a medical program; a gal from Seattle wondering where her future would take her; a blue-eyed ex-meth addict from Florida who discipled women from the red light district; my husband, Dale, a handsome, 6'3" surfer born in Hawaii and working on a PhD; and me, an Indian-born American who felt like two people in one skin, defined more by the soil under my feet, not the blood in my veins. Everyone around the table, except for Dale and me, was in his or her 20s. We added the age to create this multi-generational group.

The table was piled with food—a multi-ethnic variety to cater to multi-ethnic palates—and as always, we ate off each other's plates. Our laughter filled the night air as a full moon rose above the banyan trees. Dogs barked, and far off, we heard the cadence of a Baul folk song. It was the first week of January, and it was cool and comfortable for West Bengal, India.

It was the start of a new year, and we wanted to start it together, sharing our stories and songs and writing one-sentence goals in each other's journals. I don't remember my sentence, but I remember Dale's. It was a life changer: "I want to live with increasing reckless abandon and in constant obedience."

Three weeks later, I stood in the corner of a doctor's office in Kolkata, India. Dale had experienced strange spasms during the night, and I was concerned about his heart. I asked the doctor a question and in response he reached for a little square pad, took a pen from his pocket, and scribbled, as doctors often do, three capital letters, circled and underlined, and four words.

I didn't read the words. I just asked, "What is it?"

"It's an impossibility, a one in a million. I've never seen it. Only heard of one case in Mumbai. Your husband's heart is fine. A few of his symptoms suggest this, but I'm sure it's not."

I held the paper as we walked to our flat across the street—Dale leaning on a cane with his right hand, his left hand heavy on my shoulder.

Like a fool, I "googled" those three letters: CJD. How could three letters fill so many pages? Then I lay on Dale's computer and cried. "Jesus, don't let it be this. Not this."

Creutzfeldt-Jacob Disease, or Mad Cow Disease. Dr. Choudhury's four words to describe it: jerky movements, rapid dementia. The two words that he didn't write: imminent death.

Seventy-eight days later, Dale died—his brain making patterns like snowflakes but without the beauty, his nerves no longer carrying messages, his body convulsing to a stop. My forty-three years, ten months, and ten days as Dale's wife was over. I felt like a victim of identity theft. All the parameters and markers of my life and of who I was were gone...in one exhalation of a breath.

BEST LAID PLANS RELINQUISHED

The plans for our next few years had looked challenging but sure. We had lived much of our married life on the Indian subcontinent. We raised three children here with our third born in a jungle hospital. Now with our sons and daughter married with children of their own, Dale and I had entered a new season of investing our lives. We served on an India leadership team, and for a few years we were engaged with questions about the adjustment and training of new missionaries in a fast-changing, terror-filled world. We wrestled with strategy for reaching India's 2,000-plus unreached people groups. The solution would be a launching pad for 21st century frontier missions—a language-culture-team training location in India's Hindi and Hindu heartland.

Dale suggested we volunteer. I was irate. "What are you thinking? You can impact all of North India from where you are. Those girls in the red-light district are my unreached people group, and there are few people spending as much time in the district as I am. We speak Bengali, not Hindi. You're completing a PhD in Bengali studies, for goodness sake, and you're going to move to a place where you're hard pressed to meet a Bengali speaker?"

His answer was simple, no flair, nothing heroic or dramatic. "I'm thinking the oldest ones of us should lay down what we're doing to launch the young ones. I've never dragged you anywhere kicking and screaming, Beth, and I won't drag you here. I just think we should volunteer." He said that, climbed in bed, and went to sleep.

I climbed in bed and lay awake all night.

Since that night, I've had time to analyze my reactions to the very real war that waged inside me.

I thought about our three children and ten grandchildren and about the times I had to take something away from them. I did it one of three ways:

by force, by squeeze, or by request. By force, I can wrestle it and apply my greater strength. By squeeze, I can maneuver and apply pressure to a hand with some persuasion and cajoling. By request, I can wait for it to be placed in my outstretched hand.

In our lives, God has used all three strategies and more. There were times we moved through a wide-open door of opportunity. There were times we pushed on the door a little to release it. Other times we climbed through windows of change scrapping our elbows and knees in the process. Then there were the times a hand was placed on our head and we were pushed under a barbed wire fence with a warning: "If you keep your head down, you'll be OK. But if you pick up your head, you'll be stuck by the barbed wire, and the extraction process will be painful and not pretty. The choice is yours."

So as Dale slept, I fought. He and I played this game of sorts when God's direction seemed more difficult than the last one. I'd say, "One of these days, God will ask something so hard of me, and I'm going to say, 'No. No, I'm not up for that.'" Dale would laugh and say, "Actually, sweetheart, it doesn't work that way. Every yes that you've said to Jesus builds the foundation for the next yes. You get to the place where you've said too many yeses to say a no." Finally, at 4:30 a.m., I said yes.

Dale and I agreed to move from east to west, wet to dry, delta to desert, Bengali to Hindi, comfort and acceptance to all things new so we could be in residence at this new team site. Three weeks later, we were on the Santineketan rooftop with our multi-national friends. We dreamed possibilities: what would God do as west and east, young and old joined in a common cause—the gospel lived and proclaimed in India, the least reached nation in the world. We had flat whole wheat Indian bread and juice left over from our very common meal, and it seemed to make sense. We tore the chapattis and shared the juice remembering that the blood of the covenant is thicker than the water of the womb. We prayed for one another, grateful for this community of strangers made family, believing the next time we met, we would need a larger table.

But it was not to be. Within six weeks of our decision to move, of my very painful "yes," Dale was irrevocably sick, falling apart mentally and physically. I felt like my personhood fall apart with him.

I remember sitting outside Dale's hospital room in Kolkata. He'd been there for almost thirty days, and we were no closer to a diagnosis of the problem or how to fix it. Pastor Joti, a wonderfully prophetic prayer warrior, came to see me. She had led days of fasting and prayer for Dale's healing. She came that day to tell me that she had a dream about us and asked, "Have you released him to the Lord? Have you relinquished Dale to Jesus?"

"I think I have," I said, even as I sobbed with clenched fists.

LOSS AND GAIN

There are some interesting linguistic characteristics in the Bengali language, a language that's called the "French of the East," the language group that produces many of India's writers. In Bengali, there are compound verbs that are the same verb but in different forms and they're put back to back, like the verbs dite *(to give)* and nite *(to take)*. As compound verbs they are diye dow *("having given, release")* and niye now *("having taken, receive")*.

Elisabeth Elliot, a missionary to the Ecuadorian Amazon, returned to work with the tribe that murdered her husband Jim. She said, "Don't dig up in doubt what you planted in faith." In other words, "you gave it, now release it."

Three grown married kids and ten grandkids means that sixteen times a year, more than once a month, I have to diye dow *(having given, release)* the right and joy to be with my kids and grandkids for their birthdays. I can't seem to release it just once a year as I lay on the floor sobbing, "Jesus, I give you this birthday, this Thanksgiving, this Christmas." If I whine about it or crow about it on Facebook, it does me no good because I'm really just looking for people's pity or praise.

But it does me lots of good when I cry with the community with whom the Lord has put me, when I let them hold me up and hold me accountable to testify to God's strength in my moments of weakness.

Loss can help me live more intentionally, and gain can help me live more extravagantly. Unfortunately, my tendency in loss and gain is to just live selfishly.

When I experience loss, I make it all about me: "My losses are bigger and 'badder' than your losses." But when I live intentionally, I wake every morning and hear Jesus ask, "Beth, what are you going to do with this very short and precious life?" I find my heart reaching out to receive His daily gift of salvation and grace, but not only to receive. My life then reaches out to extend the gift so freely given to me.

When I experience gain, my flesh wants to hold it close, not wanting to share. Gain is meant to help me live more extravagantly. After Dale died, when I accepted my leader's invitation to follow through on the 4:30 a.m. "yes" to Jesus, to move and mentor young missionaries, I also made a decision that I would spend twice as much on others as I spend on myself. This helps me, as a widow on limited resources, to live giving. It's why one of my habitual sayings, when I'm asked for something is, "If I'll die for you, I'll sure share my chocolate chips with you, and my water, my washing machine, my house, my car, my money, my time, and my prayer."

One way I release *(and keep on releasing)* my life to Jesus is by writing. I think of it as a journey, as a train trip where the scenery changes, a moving from one way of thinking to another, a redefining of the terms of my life. My friends live with me when I read my journal entries to them because every time I read, I release again, and I'm reminded in what ways my loss is gain.

REDEFINING WORDS

I'm learning there are words that are cousins, and I can decide with which side of the family I identify—words like "lonely" and "alone" or phrases like "culture shock" and "cultural adaptation." If I live on the "lonely" side, there is no one who can live up to Dale and take away my loneliness, not even Jesus. If I live on the "alone" side, there are plenty of people I enjoy being with. If I live on the "culture shock" side, I'm always traumatized. If I live on the "cultural adaptation" side, I redefine the scenery, and the end result is not a straitjacket or a get-out-of-India-quick ticket.

There are times when all we can do is describe our symptoms, pain, anger, and bewilderment. Job has lived in my house for the last few years. He was in a place where God was nowhere to be found. He said, "I travel East looking for him—I find no one; then West, but not a trace" *(Job 23:8 MSG)*. I have felt that way. I've also felt what Job felt when he said, "I admit I once lived by rumors of you; now I have it all firsthand—from my own eyes and ears" *(Job 42:5 MSG)*!

This was Paul's journey: "Yes, all the things I once thought were so important are gone from my life. Compared to the high privilege of knowing Christ Jesus as my Master, firsthand, everything I once thought I had going for me is insignificant— dog dung. I've dumped it all in the trash so that I could embrace Christ and be embraced by him" *(Phil. 3:8–9 MSG)*.

That little square piece of paper that held the letters "CJD" and the words "jerky movements, rapid dementia," that paper is still with me. I carry it in the Bible that was Dale's. Part of my releasing and redefining, part of my journey is the word that Jesus spoke to me on March 10, the day the Indian doctors told us they were 90 percent sure Dale had CJD. I pounded the desk that day and moaned, "Why? Why? Why this?" I heard a response: "Beth, do you know what CJD stands for? It stands for Christ's Jurisdiction over Death."

Only Jesus can strengthen us to endure the losses. Only Jesus can redefine the words that describe our lives so loss becomes gain.

Those common table, rooftop, young friends are still part of my life, although some followed Jesus to other unreached places in the world. They love Jesus and people in Uganda, the Middle East, and American universities. Others are still in India joined by many more, each on his or her own journey to live with obedient abandonment to make the name of Jesus famous in India.

This is your invitation to pull up a chair to our common table. Come and listen .

STRANGERS BECOME FAMILY

MOVING MOUNTAINS

These days my feet are usually strapped into sturdy Columbia® walking sandals. They're not very feminine, but they're the best choice for the steep mountain roads I walk, 8,000 feet up in the Himalayas.

I don't walk these rough trails alone. There's a multi-national team of committed ones who follow me. Many are now able to keep up alongside me. There are others who run ahead, pulling me with them, navigating with youthful surety the edges of terrifying drops.

Dale always used to say, "We're living on the edge and loving it." For many years my life was a marriage. We imperfectly walked out our definition of submission. We made everything we were available to each other so that together we could be much more than either of us would be alone. God's paths in our life have been edgy paths. We experienced the thrill of successful ascent and survived the agony of, what appeared at the time, defeat.

Our story, now my story, is not the story. Yet, because of God's overwhelming grace, Jesus' bloody obedience, and the non-stop empowerment of the Holy Spirit, my story is part of God's big dream— the gospel preached to the

THOU HAST MADE ME KNOWN TO FRIENDS WHOM I KNEW NOT. THOU HAST GIVEN ME SEATS IN HOMES NOT MY OWN. THOU HAST BROUGHT THE DISTANT NEAR AND MADE A BROTHER OF THE STRANGER.

- Rabindranath Tagore, Gitanjali 63

ends of the earth. And every day again, I recognize that I stand on the shoulders of giants, that I walk in others' shoes.

My life and sacrifices are not unusual or unheard of in the kingdom story of India. Our country is full of the graves of women who came prepared to die and then did just that. India is full of the graves of godly men. The disciple Thomas was the first who worshipped Jesus as he was speared to death. I could speak of mothers burying their children— multiple children—and fathers who walked away from lucrative possibilities so they could share the riches of an eternal kingdom.

The unexpected turn in my life was a painful loss that I felt sure would finish me off. There have been a few times in the past in which I acted like the victim of a purse snatching and God was the snatcher. Now I choose instead to act as I really am—a woman who, with great freedom and for her joy, releases her life to Jesus. And there have been times I acted like God kidnapped me and brought me against my will to the places I've lived. Today, I say, "Jesus walked into the mountains of India. I just followed Him here."

I want to leave a trail of freedom in my wake. I want the people who know me well and walk alongside me to walk that trail of freedom and clear it for others to follow. We do this together, honoring the many who walked India's roads before us, who prayed for the harvest in India, who lived incredibly sacrificial lives, who joyfully died to their own desires so that the life of Jesus could take root in India.

Always we're aware that God is the One who gave us these willing feet and designed shoes for us to walk in.

STRANGERS BECOME FAMILY AT A COMMON TABLE

WELCOME TO THE WORLD

Buddhist prayer flags—blue, white, red, green, yellow—flap in the early, light breeze. I'm surprised to see them still attached after last night's storm. Heavy rain and massive wind gusts shook the thick wooden door and single-paned glass of my room. I got up multiple times through the night to close windows that popped their locks and crashed against the wall. I even jammed two old sturdy wooden spoons between the door handles concerned they, too, would fly open. Terrifying, windy storms are not unusual in this mountain region.

On the sunny, still days though, the town, spread across undulating hills with shops, schools, and houses perched on every edge, appears as peaceful as the red-robed monks who walk ascending paths with their hands clasped behind their backs. But underneath the calm of placid oriental features lies the devastation of a people forced from their Tibetan homeland. For months they hike across the snowy Himalayan range, walking at night and sleeping by day to evade border police. Children are lovingly held, kissed, and tearfully pushed out the door to make the treacherous trek to India, where they will be free to attend school in their mother tongue. We hear their stories in this Indian bazaar.

Sitting on the verandah with my Bible in hand, looking across the valley to the towering Himalayas, I nearly forget the terror of last night's storm. Morning birds sing among the budding branches. Below me the bazaar is waking, and I have a great sense of anticipation. This is my first visit. I traveled two days from my own mountain town to be here. I have come to spend a few days with a new Live Dead team. After a year of prayer walking and relationship building, and five months of searching and planning, today our multi-national, multi-generational team signs a lease on four rooms that overlook this bazaar. It's a small but significant spot, a place of welcome where friendship will be brewed as thick and hot as a cup of yak butter tea.

In this mountain town, every important, and seemingly unimportant, conversation is held over a hot drink, so you can imagine the anticipation we feel, our excitement. We've already enjoyed countless conversations over food and drink with Buddhists—students, nuns, monks, businessmen, and housewives—and at the center of each one is Jesus. He is the welcome to the world.

There are pine trees on these mountains, transplanted from their native English soil to help the British imperialists feel more at home. The trees leached the fertile earth until it could no longer support indigenous plants. These trees stand as daily reminders: the Christian religion may be a western transplant, but Jesus-life is indigenous to every language and culture.

And so with every hot pot of meat and vegetables boiled in red chili broth, with every cup of butter tea, we serve up grace and truth. We teach our taste buds to rejoice at many strange combinations so that strangers will become family at a common table.

JESUS
IS THE
WELCOME
TO THE
WORLD.

HOW TO
USE THIS
BOOK

In your hand is an invitation that is good for more than one use. This is an invitation to see strangers become family, an invitation to become a welcome to the world.

I just shared part of my story with you, and in the pages ahead I share the stories of Live Dead India teams. Live Dead is teams planting churches among unreached people groups.* I'm hopeful that as you read these stories, you will be moved to respond in new ways.

The gospel is all about access— who has access and who does not. Nearly half the world has zero access to the good news of the life, death, and resurrection of Jesus because the people don't know a single follower of Jesus. There are some who may live near Jesus-followers, but because their lives are not intertwined, there is no possibility for life-on-life transfer of truth.

Our Live Dead India teams are discovering that one of the most powerful ways to make the gospel accessible is through our lives. There was a reason why "the Word became flesh" *(John 1:14)*. We've been learning what it means to open our lives to Jesus and in turn live generous lives with neighbors and acquaintances. We're learning how to invite strangers to our common table, and in the process, see them become friends and then family. We're learning

that people often belong before they believe and that the steps of discipleship require becoming what we believe.

Over the next six weeks, we invite you to read our stories and respond to the invitations at the end of each chapter. Perhaps you will want to get together with friends and talk about your responses. Perhaps you prefer to journal on the provided pages. Either way, we are grateful that you are choosing to engage, and we believe that this process will be transformative in your life and relationships.

Each week contains five readings and concludes with a communion-breaking bread gathering. Breaking bread is best observed in a small community of friends, but as you grow in your understanding of the power of inclusion, you will see larger groups forming. Live Dead India teams often gather like this. We do it to remember the life we've received because of the life Jesus gave. We also remember together that this table is a common table—a table for the world. Please join us in becoming the welcome to the world.

WEEK ONE
prepare

day one

come

There are unique challenges to setting a table on top of a mountain. John takes on those challenges. "Someone has to do it, and it might as well be me," he says.

He is an American southern boy raised in a messy family in a town with a church on every corner and a bar on the opposite corner. John chose the bar and by 17, he was an alcoholic—hard drinking, hard living and hardworking. But then in a moment of desperation, he walked into a church, and his life changed. It wasn't the professional worship music, timely message, or ambiance that got him—it was the presence of Jesus in the middle of his brokenness.

His friends couldn't believe it, and he couldn't believe that some of his friends knew about this Jesus-life and never told him, never offered him the truth of grace, salvation, healing, and hope. How was it possible to have all that good news in one's grasp and never even mention it?

"I thought I was going to be a street preacher, because they were the most passionate, radical people I knew," he says. He attended Bible college but lived with an edge to him, at times carrying a massive wooden cross. "Someone gave me the book 'High Adventure in Tibet' and I thought, 'I could do that. From that moment on, the hills got stuck in my heart," he recalls. John's first memory of the Himalayas was a drive up a treacherous mountain road, one hairpin curve after another. "You go around a corner, the clouds lift, and you see a town on top of the hill, thousands of feet above you. It still takes my breath away."

John arrived in India, newly married. He and his bride *(Ann)* had each spent a summer interning in India while dating; their relationship was based on their mutual commitment to missions in India.

Their first home was in a north Indian city with summers so hot you stew in your own juice. Their first friends and mentors were Indian followers of Jesus, one who woke every day at 4 a.m. to pray and then traveled miles to reach the next town, the next village. John traveled with him. That context of walking with Indian friends, reaching unreached places and people, shaped the future.

John's Indian leader asked him, "Where would you like to do this?" The mountains. "We walked every day," John says, "and I was always enthralled with the mountains. You see a hundred distant villages in your view, and you know there are thousands more beyond the highest peak, a thousand more where the name of Jesus has never even been spoken. I spent as many hours as possible in the mountains. For the first few years, we had no Western

We walked every day.

friends, only backslidden Christians and few Indians who had made an initial commitment to Jesus." But slowly that changed.

Young Indian followers of Jesus heard about distant mountain villages and about a young American committed to go where there was no gospel. John knew he needed people to help him, people who could teach him how to live in India, people who knew the culture, languages, and religions. He chose to put himself with Indian brothers. He knew together they would be more effective in ministry. "We didn't need them because we wanted to take something from them. We wanted deep, trusting relationships. We began to open our home, heart, and life to Indians. We welcomed them the way they'd welcomed us. We set a table on top of the mountain where very few people had been offered the gospel, then we sat around that common table together, dreaming Kingdom dreams while sharing chapattis and dal."

Today, when John talks about his journey and his acceptance of Jesus' invitation to follow Him, he's incredulous that those with the greatest access to the truth can be the most reticent to share it. He is committed to the "come and see" gospel. He believes the only reason Jesus calls us is so we will call others.

Today, there is a table set on a mountaintop in India. The people around it are as common and as messy as John was. It's an international, multi-generational group that speaks multiple languages, includes diverse cultures and belongs to the many religions of India—followers of Hinduism, Islam, Sikhism, Buddhism, secularism, and Jesus. Some have openly accepted Jesus invitation to "come." Others are in the process—watching how we love each other, how we love Jesus, and wondering if we will love them. Our presence in their lives, the generosity of our leisurely conversation, intimate personal relationships, compassionate responses, passionate prayer, and clear proclamation of the gospel are the answer. Yes, through all these means, we will love them.

TASTE AND SEE

The loveseat and laughter is the first clue that this is more than just a kitchen. There is much more happening here than simple food preparation.

When Ann first arrived in India, a young bride fresh out of college, the phrase "a woman's place is in the kitchen" conjured up scenes of repressed females, sweat dripping off brows, relegated to back rooms for their own good, while the males, deep in weighty conversation, sat hungry and impatient to be served. But no more. She owns this space like a master chef without the arrogance and temper tantrums. She asks Pushpa to chop onions and Sherry to whip potatoes, while she mans chicken frying on the stove and Sundari washes pots and pans. Other women, young and old, Indian and American, snap green beans, hold a baby, or wait for space at the kitchen counter.

This kitchen isn't an isolated place. It is a place of community, a place that prepares the way for a larger community.

Here conversation flows. Ruchi steps forward to take a turn at the onions, giving Pushpa's eyes the chance to clear. There are reports of an unwanted infant girl found in the mountains and brought to a welcoming family. Ann asks who can give supplies immediately; then plans are made for a baby shower. Someone exclaims how many new friends are

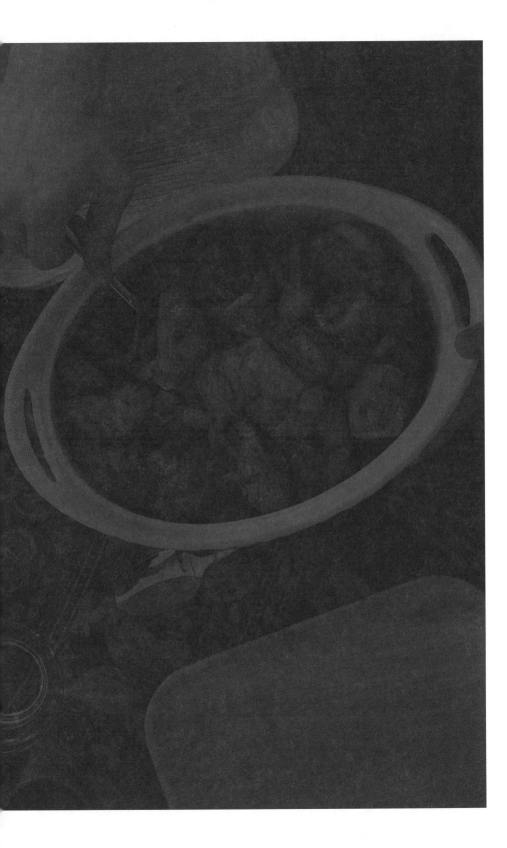

attending the CrossFit class Ann coaches. She is the queen of the plank and not half bad at burpees either. She shows the men up and is proud of it. We all laugh. Who can go with Ann tomorrow to visit a new widow who needs friends to surround her with love and prayer? We have a Thanksgiving meal to plan: vegetarian, non-vegetarian, gluten-free, Paleo, and halal. Over one hundred people will attend, the majority not followers of Jesus, but all within the growing circle of our community.

This isn't a kitchen. This is a command center.

India taught Ann to cook and to view the time and energy expended in the kitchen as much more than submission to a man. Historically, Indian women are expected to be the cooks in the family, but in today's India, this is changing, though there is still expectation that even a modern, highly educated woman will know how to cook and serve food. Parents looking for prospective brides for their sons still want to know: Does she serve tea gracefully? Did the tea taste good? Is she hospitable to guests? Ann chooses to view fulfilling these expectations as one way she can honor the cultural heritage of India, as an adaptation to become what Jesus is asking her to become. Every cup of tea she serves becomes an open door to heart-hunger. Every stomach she satisfies allows her to speak into a life, to meet the needs of the soul. This is submission to God's heart of welcome for the world.

Luke 10 recounts the story of two sisters: Martha and Mary, one who felt stuck in the kitchen and one who sat at Jesus' feet. Ann knows how to be both. She knows how to be in the kitchen with people, and she also knows how to leave the kitchen to be alone with Jesus. Both of those actions bear fruit in her life. Everywhere she lives she leads her neighbors to Jesus. She answered God's call to wholeness as a woman: serve Jesus and serve people.

Ann's prayer is: "Lord, whatever you're asking me to do, I'm going to do because I'm not just the cook in the kitchen. I'm the person providing an opportunity for many more people to come. I want people to taste and see that You are good."

DAY 3

make room

There is an obstacle ahead—a river, 50 feet wide. The method for crossing looks iffy: a metal-framed basket that's seen better days, big enough for two people if they sat knee to knee. It's attached to a rusty wire line that you hold and pull yourself across. We stood at the edge of the river weighing the risk. The goal was a village on the other side—another one-hour walk. There is also a time restraint; we need to get there before dark. We notice a spot up river that looks narrow enough to cross on foot. It seems the less dangerous option than the basket crossing, so we go for it.

John leads the way. He carries his boots over his head so they don't get wet. Boots are super important when trekking. You can be strong but then done in by blisters on your feet. John gets within ten feet of the other side and heaves his boots across. They land on the rocks. He takes a couple more steps and is suddenly over his head in rushing water. We all yell, "Come back, come back! Don't try it. The current's too strong!" John hauls himself back up, now barefoot, and our only possibility of crossing is the iffy basket and rusty wire. George Mallory, who took part in the first three British expeditions to Mount Everest in the early 1920s, said, "I climb because it's there." Now our trekking band just learned that enduring hardship requires a higher purpose. The higher the purpose, the greater the endurance, the greater the drive. For many mountain climbers, the drive is a sense of accomplishment, of putting their name on a place that only a handful of others have. Our endurance is very purposeful—people matter, people knowing the most joyful truth in the universe matters. This is why we do what we do. If I endure the next seven days, I will get to talk to someone who's never heard about Jesus. I get to put His name in a place where it's never been.

This Himalayan mountain team has gone through significant training. We walked short distances with heavy backpacks, lengthening the walk to challenge muscles to adapt and endure longer, faster, and higher. We learned that small things could deter us from the big thing, so we emptied our packs of non-essentials. John was famous for helping us decide what was essential. He could easily lighten our loads by five pounds. All those granola bars? Yeah, you can take them if you'll share them. That silk liner for your sleeping bag, forget it. You always carry that utility knife? Too bad. You need a hatchet? What, for above the tree line? You plan to lie under the Himalayan sky reading that 3-inch-thick book? Not on this trek.

When climbing at 20,000 feet, you break the handle off your toothbrush because even a small piece of plastic can be a deterrent to accomplishing a goal. The higher the altitude, the harder the trek, and the more stuff you throw out. Weight that's imperceptible at sea level feels like bricks in a backpack at 18,000 feet. "The length of the trek has very little to do with how hard a trek can be," John says. "It's what happens outside our control that's the most difficult.

And the more that's outside your control, the more choices you make about the stuff you carry."

So we all in turn climb into the rickety basket and pull ourselves across the river, and we all have cut and bloody hands by the time we reach the other side. After John retrieves boots, we climb higher toward the goal—a village that needs to hear about Jesus. The sky darkens and a flash storm unleashes torrential rain and golf ball-sized hail. Above the tree line, there was no protection. It already was cold, so now drenched and shivering, we seek shelter behind rocks. We hear the rattle, then a roar, before we see anything. An avalanche, set off by the huge hailstones, rolls toward us. We dash away from the mountainside, out into the open, and run for the bridge to the village. But the bridge is gone, washed away by flash floods.

We can't reach the village. Darkness falls, and the temperature drops more. We know we have to go back and face the basket and the wire again. We remember a village we passed four hours before the river crossing. There, also, people have never heard the story of Jesus. They also matter and reaching them becomes the new goal. Exhausted, cold, wet, hungry, we encourage each other, "Keep walking. Don't sit down." We recognize that we never would have made it this far with overweight backpacks. We're grateful we lightened our load so that we can accomplish our goal.

Dim lights flicker in the high-altitude air. We come to a house, and a woman we never met before welcomes us inside without a word or a question. She builds a fire, wraps us in blankets, and prepares rice and brown lentils, thick and hot and filling.

"WE ARE KEPT FROM OUR GOAL, NOT BY OBSTACLES, BUT BY A CLEAR PATH TO A LESSER GOAL."

- *The Mahabharata*

DAY FOUR

LEARN DEPENDI

There's nothing spiritually romantic about a five-days-a-week, 6-in-the-morning prayer meeting. How we look at 5:15 a.m. as we drag ourselves from bed is not how we want to look for public consumption. Long hair is pulled back in a ponytail, short hair covered with a hat. Makeup is non-existent. Even brushing teeth is thoroughly optional.

Our conversation at that time in the morning isn't exceptionally spiritual either. "What time did you get to bed? That late? I know it's crazy. What was I thinking?" Or, "Man, I ate something that really upset my stomach. I was running to the toilet all night."

The distance we walk to get to prayer in the morning can be a deterrent to going, too. Jumping out of bed and landing on your knees for the first hour of the day seems doable. But climbing out of bed when the room is a full 37 degrees Fahrenheit, shivering into layers of sweats and a down jacket, and then walking thirty minutes uphill or downhill to a different home each time just to meet some people to pray, that sounds torturous. It's a miracle we even do it. And the day's host of our morning prayer is up even earlier because everyone arrives looking for a cup of hot coffee or chai.

Even at 6 a.m., we are not the first ones awake and praying. The Hindu shrine gets the earliest rays of the sun as it flashes over the high Himalayas. Someone will be there to light incense and offer milk and flowers. They will pray for good results on their son's exam or for a plentiful harvest. The azaan, the Muslim call to prayer, echoes over the mountains before full daylight. "Allah is most great. Come to prayer. Prayer is better than sleep." The footsteps of the faithful respond. Buddhist monks have been sitting ramrod straight in a cold, dark temple, chanting their mantras all night long; they are way ahead of all of us. In every Indian city, town, and village, people are up early and moving toward some spiritual encounter. India is a nation of God chasers. But we know the truth: God is the real chaser, and Jesus is proof of that. He chased us down though we rebelled against Him. He continues to pursue us, each and every person in India, even when we continue to ignore His existence. Isaiah says, "I've made myself available to those who haven't bothered to ask. I'm here, ready to be found by those who haven't bothered to look. I kept saying 'I'm here, I'm here' to a nation that ignored me" (Isa. 65:1 MSG).

No one texts or knocks on doors if someone doesn't appear by 6 a.m. We're not a legalistic bunch. We are a needy bunch, though, and we come together to pray because we realize we have nothing to give. We're still learning the languages and cultures of India. We're still learning how to be the face of Jesus in this nation.

Prayer is not a posture of strength. It's our admission of weakness. Our less opens us to His more, and our prayer becomes, "Lord, do something with what I am. Make me more of what You are, so I actually have something to give." Early morning, daily prayer together as a community says, "We know we need each other, tons of grace, and the presence of Jesus if we're ever going to accomplish anything significant." Our prayer life must be a place of emptiness in order to welcome others. Togetherness in prayer is our common daily occurrence. We recognize that it's easy to pray prayers that are full of ourselves, our needs, and our wants. If we don't have room in our prayer for others, how will we have room for people at our dining room table, on our couch, or in our lives? God sets a table before us, and it has some strong brewed coffee and chai on it. It also has today's spiritual bread, which is just what we each need for faith, healing, hope, and endurance. Around the table are strangers who are now friends and family.

Ariella carries her guitar all the way to prayer, and our voices join hers. "The sun comes up. It's a new day dawning. It's time to sing your song again... Bless the Lord, oh my soul... Worship His holy name." We move into Hindi: "Yeshu tera nam, sab se ucha hai..." The name of Jesus is highest of all. We begin to pray, lifting the names of our friends, the ones with whom we committed to walk and love and live truth before, the ones we so desperately want to know Jesus.

Then invariably something happens. It has very little to do with the fire that's burning in the bokari or the mug of hot coffee warming our cold fingers. It's about our own failings and fears. It's about our grasping the truth that Jesus is indeed the God who is here, incarnate, the God who welcomes us to welcome others. Jesus didn't empty Himself of His deity when He came to earth. He emptied Himself of the prerogatives of deity. As we recognize that as individuals, it's freeing, and when we grasp it as a community, it's downright transformative.

There is something about getting empty that puts us in contact with God. As followers of Jesus, we've acknowledge our lack and neediness in the deepest way—we need salvation. Our meeting together daily for prayer is acknowledgement of our need for a Savior every day.

day five

follow the holy spirit

Joy walks off the plane clutching her pillow—old enough to want some adventure outside the safety and love of her family, hopeful enough that India will provide that, and nervous enough to feel completely out of control.

She was accustomed to urban settings after living in both Providence and Baltimore—American cities with a gritty side. She knew the gritty side of each, but neither prepared her for the in-your-face dirt and poverty of this Indian megacity.

Joy hates it and everything about it: the crowds, the smells, the bugs, the non-stop noise, and the food. She gags on papaya, the fruit served at breakfast. Without a doubt, it tastes like vomit, she says. But she really hates gulab jaman, the queen of Indian sweets and the one most likely to be served at every special occasion. She couldn't decide which was worse: the spongy texture or the sickly-sweet sugar syrup that spurted and dripped down her chin with each bite.

Joy had met missionaries from India and been challenged by their stories of desperate societal needs. She wanted to serve and do something productive with her life. Her sights were set on social work.

"Social workers have the skills to fix problems, and they know how to help people," she thought. "Plus I'm empathetic, so it seems like a good fit." She then imagined herself rescuing and counseling trafficked girls, not necessarily changing the world, but certain she could change their lives.

But here and now reality hits. There are 20 million people in extremely close proximity. It's like a paratha, or Indian fried bread, where the layers are simultaneously stuck together and slightly peeling away from each other. The stifling humidity makes her feel as if she's walking around in a sauna fully clothed. All Joy wants to do is hide away, with occasional forays into the overwhelming world of real India and real Indian lives.

In America, Joy got up in the morning, made her plans, chose what to wear, left the house when she wanted, and drove her own car to meet her friends, the ones who were most like her. On Sunday, she went to church with a pretty homogenous community. But here in India, she's stuck in a big city and told where to be and when. She navigates streets that are not on a Google map, usually from a bicycle rickshaw or a golf-cart tricycle thing, sandwiched between unfamiliar bodies, though sometimes she just takes the broken or non-existent sidewalks circumventing cows, garbage piles, and beggar kids. Some days Joy wishes for a tall, strong male to breakthrough the crowd, yell for the taxi, shield her from random stares, and give her standing in a male-dominated society. "Oh yes, that's her husband, her fiancé, or her older brother. She's not a liberal, immoral American girl. She really does have people who know her and take responsibility for her."

Eventually something starts to happen, though—partly because Jesus sent the Holy Spirit to always be with us and partly because Joy opens herself to the reality of the Spirit's presence in her. He speaks to her, leads her, and points people out to her. She learns the name of the vegetable seller at the gate of her apartment. An elderly rickshaw wallah becomes a favorite and safe driver. A young woman who is a Muslim and a clothing designer becomes a close, trusted friend who shares her problems with her. This opens the way for Joy to pray with her friend.

The Holy Spirit opens her eyes so she can see who she is in Him and how He rejoices in that, and she begins to sense His pleasure in her. Then it dawns on her that although she is not called to every single person in the city, she is called to view them as unique in His eyes. Joy now walks freely through the streets, listening to the voice of the Holy Spirit and opening her life more each day to the specific people that He brings across her path.

THE HOLY SPIRIT OPENS HER EYES.

breaking bread

R
E
A
D

↳

HEBREWS 5:7-9

GETTING OURSELVES READY

REFLECTION

- Jesus, even though He was God, showed us the way of submission to the will of God.
- Learning to pray, talking to God, listening to His voice, and sharing our deepest fears with Him are essential if we are going to be submitted to God.
- If we follow the path of God, there will be difficulties. Jesus showed us the way of submission to the will of God, even when it is costly.
- We have life today because of the willingness of Christ to lay down His life for us.
- The world that is still waiting for the gospel will not hear it until we willingly sacrifice our comfort and convenience and our safety and security so that Jesus will be made famous among all people in all the earth.

REMEMBRANCE

As you break the bread and drink the cup together today...

- Remember today Jesus sacrificed His life so that you could have life.
- Remember His sacrifice made the way for the community we have today. His sacrifice made the fellowship we share with one another possible.
- Remember the sacrifice of Christ was not just for us. His sacrifice was for all people from every tribe, every language, and every nation. Remember today those who do not know that the price of their salvation has been paid.

COMMITMENT

Today, we covenant together to life our lives as Jesus lived. Jesus, You gave everything to that everyone could have life. We pledge our lives today to live only to make Your name famous in all the earth. We know we cannot do this in our own strength and commitment. Jesus, we ask You to give us the grace we need to follow Your example. As You lived Your life, not for Your own self, but for the will of the Father, help us that we would not live our lives for ourselves, but for You and those for whom You gave Your life.

WEEK 1, DAY 1

An invitation to come.

Jesus is inviting you to join him in a lifestyle of adventure.

Will you come?

_____

_____

_____

_____

_____

_____

_____

_____

_____

_____

_____

_____

WEEK 1, DAY 2

An invitation to be.

Jesus is inviting you to be present where you are and where you go. Sometimes that means even being present when the circumstances aren't what you had envisioned or in a place you feel stuck.

Where are you going to choose to be present today?

_____

_____

_____

_____

_____

_____

_____

_____

_____

_____

_____

WEEK 1, DAY 3

An invitation to let go.

Jesus is inviting you to let go of everything that is weighing you down or keeping you from freely stepping into your adventure with him.

What do you need to let go of today?

_____

_____

_____

_____

_____

_____

_____

_____

_____

_____

_____

WEEK 1, DAY 4

An invitation to start the day together.

Jesus is inviting you to start the day with him. Maybe you don't have a 6 a.m. prayer meeting you can attend, but you can focus your first thoughts toward God when you step out of bed each day.

How can you change your morning routine to bring your mind and heart first to a conversation with Jesus?

_____

_____

_____

_____

_____

_____

_____

_____

_____

_____

WEEK 1, DAY 5

An invitation to walk in the Spirit.

Jesus is inviting you to allow His Spirit to guide your day, maybe even to uncomfortable places.

Where may be asking you to go today that takes you out of your comfort zone? Invite the Holy Spirit within you to guide you there.

invite the holy spirit

week two
welcome

The door to their flat just stays open. Actually, there's little chance for it to close with the steady stream of guests arriving for the third annual Friendsgiving dinner. The table is full of vegetarian, non-vegetarian, and halal dishes, each clearly marked. Bradley and Jane met many of their guests in an art museum or music venue around this city that is a cauldron of creativity. There were meetings over coffee, visits to businesses or studios for more conversation, and finally an invitation to their home for a meal.

Bradley loves India, and he love this city with all its creative energy. But he loves the people more and loves getting to know the details of their lives. If his new friend is an artist, he wants to know what inspires them to create their art. If a musician, what drives them to write, sing or play? In the West, we experience the individualistic side of the arts: "this is my thing," "my art," or "my music." But in India the scene is different; it's more collaborative. There are deep conversations about how art opens our lives to people and how art reveals the inter-connectedness of individuals and communities.

Bradley and Jane think collaboration is one of the strengths of India and have started to think that we're not meant to do things alone. For an Indian, there's almost no difference in the definition of family and community—one easily flows into the other. An individual person is separate and not separate at the same time. It's like a pashmina shawl in which the individual threads are distinguishable but have no beauty, form, or function without being woven together with threads of other colors. Bradley and Jane are learning family, community, and collaboration from their artistic Indian friends.

But in all honesty, these friends are a challenging group of people. They challenge the norms of Indian society. Many experiment with drugs and alcohol, and with some it's not just experimentation, it's a way of life. Their belief systems keep them on the broken edge of healthy and whole relationships. Promiscuity is rampant. Because people are messy, relationships are messy. Bradley and Jane are learning to expect messy and to not turn away from it. They're learning how to do life together with people who are not all followers of Jesus in all the good, the bad, the joys, and the sorrows. Artists are especially sensitive to the troubles around them in the world, and that sensitivity means that they also feel the peace and centeredness of Bradley and Jane's lives. When the artists hang out with a whole team that lives with Jesus as their center, it has a strong effect on them. Through every conversation, every art show, every coffee, and every event, the team carries the presence of God.

Tonight is no different. Friendsgiving is proof that with Jesus there are no outsiders. We welcome all because He welcomed all. It's like the story in Luke 5: "Levi gave a large dinner at his home for Jesus. Everybody was there, tax men and other disreputable characters as guests at the dinner" (v. 29 MSG). When the Pharisees and scholars questioned Jesus' disciples, "What is he doing eating and drinking with crooks and sinners" (v. 30)? Jesus says, "Who needs a doctor: the healthy or the sick? I'm here inviting outsiders, not insiders—an invitation to a changed life, changed inside and out" (v. 31–32).

THEY'RE LEARNING HOW TO DO LIFE TOGETHER.

SATISFIED

Long before the sun rises, dawn arrives. At first, the sky is so black that her eyes can barely differentiate a snow mountain from a green mountain. But soon the edges of dark hulks lighten like an oil lamp glowing through a teacup made of amber. The birds know it's coming. Tsampa barley porridge boils on a single burner propane stove, and the aroma of hot liquid ghee preparing to drench a paratha makes her mouth water. A dog scratches himself awake and walks toward the promise of food.

Jean is learning to apprehend the signs of light and life in the dark. It's all very new to her. When she first felt the claustrophobia from a crowd of burgundy clad nuns and was first greeted "tashi dalay" in a strange tongue and first watched a gnarled hand pushing beads between wrinkled fingers while lips moved in a soft mantra to ward off demon spirits, she was only aware of the dark. When she first joined devotees as they circumambulated the temple and first watched prostrations more difficult than CrossFit planks and first heard deep guttural chanting, she only sensed heaviness, like muscles so sore you can't lift them.

But she's changing. Everyday Jean learns to abide in Jesus and greet suspicious glances with a smile like

Jesus. "One of the things I've learned from my Buddhist friends is to just live life with people," she says, "I want to become better at that, at setting aside my schedule." That's not something we see much in the flow of American life, but she continues to learn that simply allowing people into her life is important. And she recognizes that this is part of Jesus' appeal to people—He took time to talk with people, walk with people, and eat with people. So, every time Jean pours ginger lemon tea for an acquaintance or invites her friend Dolma to eat with her, she becomes more and more aware. Jesus is drawing people to Himself, and she is

the appetizer.

She becomes less and less afraid of the questions about her life, her goals and her beliefs. In fact, she welcomes them because they deepen conversation and deep conversations are windows to soul hunger. The other day she sat with Dolma in a local café where they drank tea together and talked about all kinds of things. Dolma asked if she liked poetry, and there was an instant connection. Jean's favorite poem is "The Road Not Taken" by Robert Frost. She summarized her favorite stanza, which says that choosing to take the more difficult road makes all the difference. Dolma noted that there

is an ancient Chinese proverb that shares the same idea: when offered two roads, choose the more difficult one. To which Jean replied, this is also in the teaching of Jesus: the easy, wide path leads to destruction, but the narrow, more difficult path leads to joy *(Matt. 7:13–14)*.

Then Jean and Dolma talked about a recent visit by His Holiness, the Dalai Lama. According to Dolma, one thing he emphasized was that Buddhists were not doing a good job of having compassion on those around them. He encouraged people to look to true believers in Christ as examples. He pointed out that followers of Jesus care for people, while most Buddhists

focus on earning karma for their next life. Jean replied that this is because Jesus tells us the most important commandments are two things: to love God and to love people. Dolma exclaimed, "This is a wonderful teaching," agreeing that these are the two most important things. "I'll never forget the way she smiled at me as she said, 'I think I'm still in the process of choosing my path,'" Jean said.

Jean knows what it means to hunger for God's Word, but now finds herself voraciously reading with an appetite she barely knew was possible: "Jesus is my Bread of Life, more dense and delicious than Tingmo steamed Tibetan bread." Jesus' words are true: "It takes more than bread to stay alive. It takes a steady stream of words from God's mouth.

If I make you light-bearers, you don't think I'm going to hide you under a bucket, do you? I'm putting you on a light stand." *(Matt. 4:4; 5:15)*.

Those are words that had to be translated, extrapolated, and explained before she lived in India. But now each time the electricity goes off unexpectedly and she lights a candle or an oil lamp and places it on the table, Jean understands anew. She tastes faith. Hope and possibility are more than flickering flames. Spiritual hunger is a shared human experience, and as she becomes more aware of it in herself, she is more open to its expression in others.

day three

forgiven

We jumped from the auto rickshaw into the middle of traffic and ignored the blaring horns. She protectively takes my hand and leads me across the busy street weaving between buses, cars, motorcycles, and rickshaws. "Stay close," Jamuna says. I'd been here many times before and walked past the stinking men's urinals, holding my breath and averting my eyes, but because today I came at her request as her guest, she feels the need to take care of me.

Twenty-four hours a day, this place is crowded and it takes no imagination to know why. A Mardi Gras atmosphere prevails—loud music, the aroma of fried foods, the odor of sweat, and the women with eyes and lips painted to draw attention. Their faces look much too old or incredulously too young. My reaction, as always, is to feel slightly sick to my stomach.

She continues to hold my hand, quickly moving through the crowd, turning down one lane after another. Each turn brings us into narrower spaces where curtained doors open to the alley. I don't want to look. I don't want to see the vacant stares and painted smiles of pre-pubescent girls leading customers inside.

Jamuna is a strange combination, an enigma: both a part and not a part of the red-light district. She was sold into this place as a young girl. She endured physical and mental torture and believed there would be no end to her suffering. Her closest relationship was with a man she called her "babu," her pimp. But today she has many friends. Some are women who were sold and are now free—but not just free from the control of others or a way of life, but ransomed, redeemed, and forgiven.

FORGIVE

Jamuna is ecstatic. A friend visited Tripura and returned with homegrown fruits and vegetables, so she has something to share. The other women in the vocational center bring their lunches, and we sit on brightly colored woven mats as tin tiffin boxes pass between us. In the past Jamuna's offering was often sparse—a few tablespoons of spinach fried with garlic and onions, and some whole-wheat chapattis—but she gave what she had and longed to give more.

GIVE

She reaches for the key swinging at the end of her dupatta *(a shawl)*. By the size of that lock, one would think there were valuables behind the door. A single bulb, hanging from a long cord, gives off a dim light to

LIGHT

the interior. The plain cement floor is swept clean; a jharu *(broom)* stands by the door. The three-quarter bed is neatly made with pillows and quilts folded. It's against the wall of cracked plaster stained black with soot and green with mold. A round, deep, red, clay pot holds drinking water; beside it are two tin cups and two plastic plates. There is a single-burner propane stove and a collection of old bottles of spices. In the center of the floor sets a rough, bulging burlap bag.

HOME

She finally releases my hand long enough to pat the bed and invites me to make myself at home. She chatters away and asks me how sweet I want my chai. She fills her single pan with water from the clay kolshi *(pot)* and adds some milk. As it boils, she releases a fistful of tea leaves from an old jar and another handful of sugar. The deep aroma of strong black tea fills the tiny room as she pours it through a chai chakni *(tea strainer)* into my tin cup. "You won't have?" I asked. "No, no auntie. First see."

With that, she upends the burlap bag, and laughs and claps like a child who just spilled her Legos. Mangoes, potatoes, onions, and squash roll across the floor and under the bed. Then methodically, she divides her treasures into three piles: one for a friend in the red-light district, one

JOY

for me, and the smallest for herself. The joy on her face is palpable. Turning suddenly, she slaps her hands on my knees. "Auntie, how did God find me down in this dark place?"

I am taken aback by her question, surprised by the clarity. "God is in all the dark places, Jamuna. He's always looking for us. Only some people turn around and see Him."

LOOKING

"I turned around," she says.

DAY FOUR

TRANSF

"I wouldn't be here today without their welcome." That sounds like a pretty extreme statement, but the pure, intense expression on his dark, handsome face makes me listen. Tanuj hands me the best cup of hot chai, cinnamon sprinkled around the foaming edge, then settles into a comfortable rattan chair across the wooden coffee table from me. We're sitting in the corner of an amazing café. The blackboard wall behind my head is covered with words of affirmation from satisfied customers in Hindi and English.

It is a March morning and still relatively cool. Bright sun shines through wide windows to our left that look out on a two-lane road. A herd of cows meander up a slow incline of the mountain.

"My mom was pregnant with me. She wasn't married. My biological father married my mother's best friend, and they lived 200 meters from us. I have no memory of my father ever acknowledging me or ever helping my mother. She worked as a maid." When he uses that word, I know he doesn't mean it in the American context. "She carried water for 50 rupees a day and leftover food. My mother was also responsible for her two brothers and grandmother. I hated the poverty. I had a grudge against my mother because she didn't give me enough. My friends had money, and I didn't. I dreamt of leaving home, of becoming wealthy. No one would be able to look down on me then. When you have money, people don't care about your history.

"We lived in the middle of a large Christian community of over 5,000 families. There are few places like that in India. I was one of those Christians who went to church on Christmas day but was drunk by evening. Depression hounded me. I was only sober long enough to procure more alcohol or more drugs. I went through a six-month period of time when I barely slept. My life and habits

were intense, even violent. I couldn't stay out of fights and thought nothing of slapping women around.

"Then I hit the jackpot. I won 8,000 rupees gambling. I bought a bus ticket for the 1,000-kilometer trip from my home to Bangalore, the city of my dreams. Many of my friends moved to Bangalore and gotten jobs working in call centers or multi-national companies. They assured me I could find a job, too. In Bangalore, you have to know English well or you'll never get a job. I gave interviews but couldn't even introduce myself. I failed again and again. They encouraged me to learn Spanish, and it appeared that I had an aptitude for the language. Finally, I got a job translating medical documents from Spanish to English. "But my addictions followed me, and my alcoholic friends didn't help. I can't tell you the nights that at 1 a.m., I'd troll all the paan (a drug) shops, picking up pieces of cigarettes off the ground, desperate for some kind of a high. In the middle of growing success at work on the one hand and insurmountable addictions on the other, I got a text message from a young woman from school. She asked how I was doing. She was from a well-respected family who were true followers of Jesus. We stayed in touch, texting, and she encouraged me to go to church. I still couldn't stop my bad habits; they had been my constant companions for sixteen years. I started to read the Bible, crying out to Jesus for help. The first book I read was 1 Corinthians. I thought that the only bad thing in me was my addictions, but I began to see that God had to forgive me and heal me of so many things.

"My texting friend and I began to talk about marriage, but when she told her family, they were disturbed and angry; they knew my reputation. But over time they heard about the transformation in my life. Her brothers met me and finally agreed to a wedding. Marriage to Anu is the biggest blessing in my life, and now God has given us a son. I'm learning to be a true husband and father. Anu's family has welcomed me as their own son and here at the café I have a community of friends who surround me. They show me what it means to walk with Jesus. Every day I'm overcoming and leaving my past behind. Now everyone in my society respects me, and my mother is also respected.

"Every single day I remind myself that this is the real world and the people I meet in this café are real people, many who need Jesus. Here I look after the compost and the garden and manage the finances for the café. Whatever God asks me to do, He gives me the resources I need. Besides learning the Bible, I'm learning to respect people. Respect is important because it opens up people to me. I'm growing every day. I don't think I can preach, but I can do a good job and show people respect.

"I'm learning the transforming power of a welcome."

day
free

freed

Balram bathed and put clean clothes on after fasting for the entire day. Neighbors had been arriving for hours, crowding the family home, and the drums had already started their incessant beat.

He is afraid and has no desire to go inside the stone house with the gabled slate roof. Other mountain houses are scattered for almost half a mile across the southeast contour of a hillside overlooking the mountains and valleys of the Garhwal, "but all of my fear centers on this particular house, this place that should be the safest place on earth to me."

Balram's journey to this moment began nearly four years ago. That was the first time he passed out, fainted dead away at school. After that, he experienced vertigo and would suddenly lose consciousness. It never came at any particular moment. He might be sitting at his school desk, walking the high, narrow path between school and home, or playing with friends. Balram's parents felt helpless, afraid that he would die. His mother would go to the corner of their house where the altar to their family gods stood. She burned incense and offered special food that she cooked with pure ghee or milk. For three or four days, Balram moved in and out of consciousness, too weak to even use the toilet or feed himself.

His parents finally decided that he would leave school. They couldn't take the chance that he might fall on the five-kilometer trail between the village and school, and there was no hospital in the village. In fact, there was no hospital for miles. Fear became his constant companion, and spiritual darkness suffocated him. Balram was surrounded by hopelessness, fear of death, and fear of the gods and goddesses; everything was overwhelming, controlling fear.

Balram's oldest brother, Madesh, was a follower of Jesus. He rarely visited, but he left a New Testament at their home. With nothing better to do, Balram began to read. The birth of a God-man, a virgin birth, was a new idea, but what gripped him and wouldn't let go were the stories of healing. Who was this God who cast out demons with a word and healed a woman who had bled for twelve years or a man who was sick for thirty-eight years? And raising the dead and healing lepers, how was that possible? His family had so many deities, but they never heard of them healing or raising people from the dead. Balram began to wonder, "Is this only a story book?" Then he found a magazine with modern stories of Indian people meeting with God, and he began to feel that Jesus was real and was a God who could help him.

Meanwhile, his parents visited the soothsayer in another village to ask about Balram's condition. His answer was, "Your family gods are unhappy. You need to please them by offering expensive food and fruits. You need to offer sacrifices." His parents borrowed money from family members and friends to provide for the gods. The soothsayer also told them that a new deity wanted to join their family but needed an invitation to possess Balram. "He'll possess Balram, and Balram will dance and prophesy. This is a great honor. After that, Balram will be healed."

The day arrives. This is the day the priest decided would be the most auspicious day for the ritual, and now everyone waits inside for Balram. He turns to his mother and says, "I'm afraid. I don't want to go

inside." "We're doing this so that you will live and not die," she replies. The drums beat. The fire burns bright, and the priest begins the rituals, burning wheat, barley, and ghee in the fire. The priest then sings and chants and calls the spirit to come. Other spirits begin to possess the people, and they begin to dance and come toward Balram, touching and shaking him, pulling his hair and clothes. He starts to shiver. In his heart, he begins to call on Jesus, "Save me! Save me! If You're the true One, the only true God, stronger than these, then save me today."

An intense hour passed, and at one point, Balram thought, "I'll give up to the spirit and let it possess me."

Suddenly, the people dancing around him looked tired. As they come back to themselves, they slump to the floor. The priest stops chanting, and the drums stop beating. The priest now feels that he has nothing stronger to call on to make the spirit come to Balram, and he announces to his parents that he was finished. "There's a mighty power blocking the spirit's arrival. It's all around Balram. The spirit can't get through it."

Balram is ecstatic. Jesus has saved him from possession. To top it off, his mother and father turn and say, "Today is the last day that we will worship these deities."

breaking
bread

R
E
A
D

1 CORINTHIANS 11:17–29

NO
OUTSIDERS

REFLECTION

- **Paul corrected the churches that were missing communion.** Communion was meant to show our restored relationship with Christ and with one another. By eating alone, they missed the whole purpose.

- **Everyone is welcome.** Christ has prepared a place at the table for all of us. Not all have received Jesus, but He is willing to receive us all if we will only believe and call on His name.

- **Remembering Jesus is the key to communion**—remembering that He not only died for me, but He also died for us, the body of Christ, and for them, those not yet at the table.

- **To eat in an unworthy manner is to eat thinking only of ourselves** and not thinking of our brothers and sisters in Christ and those who have never heard.

- **Remembering requires examining ourselves:** am I doing everything I can do with everything Christ has given me to make sure everyone knows they have a seat at the table?

REMEMBRANCE

As you break the bread and drink the cup together today...

- **Remember you are at the table because Jesus prepared a place for you.**

- **Remember to never eat alone.** Communion is a celebration of relationship. The restored relationship we have with the Lord and with one another.

- **Remember those who are not at the table today.** Friends, family members, co-workers, classmates, and neighbors who are not following Jesus. Remember the over 1.3 billion people of India representing over 2,000 unreached people groups who are not at the table today.

COMMITMENT

We covenant today, Lord, to never eat alone. You have created us for community. We come to the table today remembering the wonderful fellowship You have given us with You and with one another. We commit our lives today to spreading the news that You have prepared a place at the table for all people.

WEEK 2, DAY 1

An invitation to welcome.

Step out and invite someone who isn't in relationship with God and who may live differently than you to a meal. This could be someone who you already have a relationship with or someone you meet for the first time.

Who are you going to welcome to the table?

_____

_____

_____

_____

_____

_____

_____

_____

_____

_____

_____

_____

_____

WEEK 2, DAY 2

An invitation to live life together.

Yesterday you stepped out to welcome someone to your table. Think about your life as a whole and with whom your path crosses on a normal week.

How can you be more intentional in the rhythm of daily life to care for these people?

_____

_____

_____

_____

_____

_____

_____

_____

_____

_____

_____

_____

WEEK 2, DAY 3

An invitation to step in.

This week so far you've been intentional to step out, welcome, and care for others on your path. Today, step into someone's life who could use encouragement. Rather than waiting for them to accept your invitation, be present with them where they are, even in their mess.

Into whose life are you going to step?

_____

_____

_____

_____

_____

_____

_____

_____

_____

_____

_____

WEEK 2, DAY 4

An invitation to speak life.

We have been connecting outwardly, along our path, and stepping intentionally into someone's life this week. Take a moment to pray for each of these people in whom you've committed to invest and send them some words of truth. It could be as simple as an encouraging text or a quick phone call to ask them how they are.

Respond thoughtfully and prayerfully to them.

_____

_____

_____

_____

_____

_____

_____

_____

_____

_____

_____

WEEK 2, DAY 5

An invitation to freedom.

Think about the things that keep you from truly living freely with God. Take some time today to talk to God and embrace the freedom He gives. As you connect at the table with others, invite them to do the same.

In what area are you embracing Christ's freedom today?

live freely with god

week three
authenticity

day one

from broken to whole

He walks toward her table carrying a goldfish bowl. Three bright orange little guys swim around and around. "So you won't be alone," he says to her as he sets the bowl in the center of the table. There is no Hindi word for "privacy." If Renee describes herself as a "private person" or an introvert, many Indians are appalled. The word akela means "alone," but the real meaning is "lonely," a feared concept in this land of 1.3 billion people, where everyone is known by her or his relationships.

Renee remembers sitting on the top floor of a mall, completely alone, eating an ice cream cone. There was not one person within earshot, no one in sight. It was wonderful. There were numerous empty benches in the area. Eventually a large group of young Indians came up and sat near her. Then one young lady left the group, came over, and sat, not on a nearby bench, but on Renee's bench. And not just on the bench, but right next to her, almost touching her. It felt strange, but in the young Indian's mind, it was the only kind thing to do. No one wants to sit and eat alone in India.

Many times, Renee wonders if she is the kind of missionary Jesus needs in India, feeling as if she's not enough. She doesn't question her commitment or calling, but she has questioned if her personality, background, and gifts are sufficient. Her earliest memories are her mother reading to her from a big, blue Bible storybook, and she knows there must be a moment when she started to love Jesus, but she can't pinpoint the moment. She remembers her water baptism at 10, but her relationship with Jesus far preceded that formality.

Renee married and moved with her husband to Alaska. It's possible the wide and wild expanses of Alaska suited her. She served alongside her husband as youth pastor and senior pastor before they became missionaries to South America. It was there that their marriage began to fall apart. "Although looking back I see the signs of brokenness long before that," she says. Years of ministry experience did not prepare her for separation and divorce or for the pain and devastation in the lives of her children. And yet her heart still longed for the unreached places in the world, and she still dreamed of speaking the name of Jesus to people who never heard of him.

But now she feels unworthy. She knows the biggest challenge is her internal struggle as she works through shame, failure, lack of self-worth, and self-confidence, and she knows she needs to find herself as a whole person in Jesus. She realizes she needs to figure out who she is as an individual. She had always known herself as someone's daughter, wife, or mother. As she went through the approval process for missions once again, she found herself falling through what she calls "every crack possible." Through the process,

she learned how to deal with being overlooked or not being taken seriously and what it felt like to be "treated like a woman" without a man standing beside her any longer. Apart from the grace and goodness of Jesus, she might not have persevered.

Renee is grateful that she did persevere. She's learning to be less introverted for the sake of relationships with people who need to know the life of Jesus. She no longer needs a bowl of goldfish to keep her company because her table is more and more a common table with friends gathered. Today she leads a multi-national team of adventurous and committed young ones whose whole heart is to reach Tibetan Buddhists living in India. She recognizes that the experiences that broke her are the very experiences that help her as she lives among a people who themselves experienced brokenness and homelessness, as their nation of Tibet was occupied by a foreign power. God gives her gifts of intercession and leadership, and dreams and plans for business platforms that open doors for life to flow to people who themselves live broken and lonely.

"GOD TO BE GOD MUST RULE THE HEART AND TRANSFORM IT."

- Mahatma Gandhi

WEEK 3 / DAY 2: AUTHENTICITY

FROM NEED TO GENEROSITY

It's hard to imagine Usha making moonshine. I also can't see her carrying rocks on her head for retaining walls and roads, although she looks sturdy and resolute enough to do both. Today, she wears a flowing, blue salwar kameez, a knee-length shift with wide pants underneath, and a scarf draped around her neck. Usha's wide face is set in a perpetual grin. Her white teeth flash and long earrings jingle as she throws back her head and laughs.

She places small bowls overflowing with Punjabi tadka namkeen on the massive wooden table and returns with two trays of chai—one with sugar and one without. It's three weeks before Easter, and some around the table gave up sugar for Lent. Others are fasting rice, so by this time in the evening they are feeling uncomfortably empty. Rice is the twice-a-day staple of their diet. Multiple hands reach for the cups and scoop up a handful of salty namkeen to eat alongside. In India, snacks always accompany chai—cookies or a variety of spicy fried noodles, mixed with peanuts.

Twelve people settle onto long benches on either side of the table— all married couples, five Indian and one American. Amreeta and Lopsang each hold their infant sons, swaying gently to help them sleep. Five more children sit at the ends of the table, chattering in Hindi. Two of the boys are fair-skinned, but as you hear them speak, you would not peg them as Americans.

Rohit strums the guitar, tightening the strings, and then plays a familiar tune, humming the first bars. Others join him, softly at first, then with more intensity as the words take hold of their hearts, rising in the night air, joining evening birds and crickets. "You are my mercy-giving Lord. You are my forgiveness-giving Lord. And I have given You nothing." Usha's voice is the loudest; she sings with abandon at the top of her lungs.

One man reads in Hindi from John 8, the story of the woman caught in the act of adultery. "The sinless one among you, go first: Throw the stone" (v. 7 MSG).

The past two days were difficult at the café, a business that provides relationship-building opportunities in this majority Hindu city. A neighbor stormed into the café, disrupted business, caused embarrassment, and accused someone of stealing a cell phone. Every attempt to speak truth and peace into the situation backfired, and finally the police were called. There was a demand for a written apology, delivered to the perceived wronged party at the police station in front of witnesses. Everyone from the café is smarting at the open shame and injustice. They are a community committed to treat each customer with kindness and respect—from the Class 10 student or the Bollywood actor to the important government official. The café is known for excellent food, service, and ambiance, and local workmen know them to be fair and just. Now around the table the words from John 8 grip their hearts. None of them are sinless, Usha included.

Usha loves the acceptance and stability she receives from this kingdom community. She was married to a cruel man, an alcoholic, who forced her to make illegal liquor and carry rocks to support his habit.

It went on for years. She had borne him a son and survived his abuse. She lived in a village on a path frequented by trekkers, so to earn a little more income, she would cook a meal with food they provided or offer space on her floor to sleep. She shared what she had, and in the process, words of life and water to her soul were shared with her. She desired to support her child and herself but not by making moonshine, which had destroyed her husband's life. The opportunity presented itself for a new life with a family that took her as their own, a community of believers in Jesus that walk with her on the road of redemption. She jumped at the chance and now grows in faith. Her faith is marked by generosity. She no longer sees herself as needy and empty-handed. She takes every opportunity to cook, serve, visit the sick, and help orphans, grateful to be able to share.

Usha prays: "Jesus, we are all people who had nothing, and most of all we did not know peace and forgiveness. We didn't deserve either. I didn't deserve either. Give me grace to give what You gave to me."

from grief to comfort

day three

One particular January was the first time in her whole life that she was painfully honest with her parents. She told them that for years she had systematically lied to them. The very next month, her dad was diagnosed with pancreatic cancer. February is a very cold, dark month in Minnesota.

Although Sara was raised in a nominal Christian home, she knows she was not a true follower of Jesus. It took a move to Hawaii after college, and some pretty radical roommates for that transformation to happen in her life. She spent the first month of this new year with her parents, the first significant amount of time at home since she came to faith. She knew it wouldn't be easy, but she knew she had to come clean. "I had to be honest with them about all the bad stuff I'd been into in my years growing up," she says. She confessed all her lies to her mom and dad, and they were shocked. They couldn't imagine how out of touch they were, but they forgave her. It was an enormously freeing and healing time for Sara.

And then the news arrived—dad had cancer of the pancreas. She admits that if she had known about the cancer before, she's not sure she would have had the courage to confess her old life to her parents. But she also knows that she would not have had the freedom to move into the new life that Jesus prepared for her.

Sara had served for a couple years in Laos and loved it. She taught English, learned Lao, made deep friendships, and saw many friends come to faith in Jesus. But then a new opportunity came: India. At first she could not imagine making the move. It made little sense—until the Lord reminded her of a journal entry in which she wrote about a recurring dream. In the dream, she was traveling and kept overshooting her destination, arriving in a city with red-roofed buildings. She knew that Jesus often spoke to her through dreams, and she also knew that the city in which the India team asked her to live was full of corrugated tin roofs...painted red.

Sara's dad underwent major surgery to lengthen his life. The family was told there was no cure, just the possibility of a few more months. They removed his gall bladder, spleen, and pancreas, but a sudden bowel obstruction landed him back in the hospital. The wound from his surgery wouldn't heal. It was wide open. It was horrific. Eventually, the family brought him home and cared for him. Sara and her sister committed to feed him healthy food, and it seemed to make a difference. He grew stronger and started gardening and golfing, the things he loved to do in a Minnesota summer. They began to hope, thinking God healed him.

Sara moved forward with her planning to move to India, but the family was suddenly shaken when her grandmother unexpectedly died. Sara was in the middle of her training with her eyes set on India and her heart broken for home. At the end of summer, in August, her dad grew sick again. By October, the prognosis was the unthinkable—he was full of cancer and would likely never eat again.

Sara remembers Thanksgiving that year. Her family went to an aunt's house, grateful that her dad could come home from the hospital. A tall man and a doctor himself, her dad was once strong, active, proud, and in control. But now, "he was a shadow of the father I'd known," she says. He so desperately wanted to eat some of the celebratory meal; he may have managed to swallow a tiny forkful of food. Sara thought for sure his death would come quickly, but he surprised them, living on fluids for two more months. In December her father made peace with death. Sara's parents regularly attended church during her childhood, but they started to follow Jesus more closely after they visited her in Hawaii. "I'm sure they saw the transformation in my life," she says. Later, when she moved to Laos, they visited again, and she knows it had an impact on them. But in the end her dad would say, "Cancer healed my life." The realization that he was not in control of his own breath opened him up to the Author of Life. His Bible became his constant companion, along with the physical pain that was agonizing for him to endure and for the family to watch.

That's when Sara's dilemma became real. She wondered, "Should I leave for India now or not?" Half of her just wanted to get out of there. Her move would not change the outcome, and it's hard to watch a father die. The other half of her wanted to stay, to be with her mother and sister and to live these final painful days together. Her dad could speak until the last week of his life. He decided to stop drinking water, and as a doctor, he understood that without fluids the end would come more quickly. No one understood how his body held on; he was literally skin and bones. By now everything was in place for Sara to leave for India, and early on the morning of February 17, her dad left. Two months later, she left, too.

Sara arrived in India and joined a team with significant experience in loss. It included other women who had lost fathers. Straightaway, there was a definite bond. They cried together and shared stories and books that held them steady, even as they studied language, learned culture, and began to build Indian friendships. Eventually Sara's birthday came around, and at her birthday party, different friends shared stories about her. Balay, one of her Sikh friends, said, "Sara and I have a bond we share. We share the death of our fathers."

Sara says that one discovery surprises her: she believes if she stayed in the U.S., she would have felt more comforted through her loss, but by coming to India, she found friends who helped her heal. Even people who don't yet follow Jesus are sensitive to her feelings and ask questions about her family's death-journey. Their tenderness to her helps her become more like that with others. She feels more sensitive to people who are grieving any kind of loss, and she feels more compassionate for people who are suffering painful sicknesses.

She still gets asked, "What are you running away from?" Her answer is: "I'm not running away from anything. I'm moving forward. I'm learning to have Jesus' heart for India. I've spent much of my life trying to figure out what people want from me and trying to please people, but God is breaking me of that. Grieving is real and necessary, and my father's death is also teaching me to view my life more in the scope of eternity."

from speechless to life words

Learning Hindi is difficult. Some people find it almost effortless and excel at speaking the language, but knowing that makes it more difficult for Meri. Her first language experience was with three twenty-somethings. It seemed to her that they could hear a word twice and remember it forever, while she in her early fifties used every power of concentration, 3x5 vocabulary cards, and voice recordings, but could not retain a word she heard a dozen times. Her frustration was constant.

Meri is a confident, self-reliant, and optimistic woman, a CEO with years of experience communicating important information to a wide range of employees. And yet here she is with a strong desire to communicate the most life-changing message in the history of the universe, and she feels like a 2-year-old blubbering baby talk in front of kind, and sometimes not so kind, Indian faces smiling condescendingly at her.

Anyone raised in a Pentecostal church knows the missionary stories of language miracles, and Meri just wants her miracle. She wants to walk into the red-light district of her city and speak truth, new life, and forgiveness to sex-trafficked women. She wants to speak with kindness because they experience hatred. She wants to speak with clarity because their lives are full of confusion. She wants to speak with unconditional love because within every woman is a little girl who wants to be truly loved. All of those powerful, biblical concepts take language skills far beyond her ability in Hindi.

Now here she is enrolled in Hindi classes for a second time. Once again, surrounded by young learners, she plows her way through class determined that she will not leave in tears and that she will complete the course with the fluency needed to do the work of Jesus. He prepared her in so many other ways, including giving her a compassion for people like she'd never experienced before. Brokenness and poverty are everywhere in India. Before Meri lived here, she was generous to the poor, but she never felt moved by their need.

But now that feeling was visceral. She was much more empathetic than apathetic. Her empathy became part of her motivation to learn Hindi; it was also a motivation to rescue trafficked girls. What these girls needed was to get out of that horrible place! But then one day Meri spoke with Anu, a 12-year-old girl who was being sent to the red-light district in Mumbai. The decision was made; it would not be changed. Anu knew what was in store for her; she knew because she'd heard stories from others sent there. In simple faith that put Meri to shame,

Anu spoke words of life, "I know that Jesus goes with me."

Back in Hindi class, they are studying past, present, and future tenses, and Meri is not getting it. She feels more and more like a failure as a missionary and even worse as a person. She barely makes it through the class. As soon as she leaves, the tears just start flowing. At that moment, she realizes she can be in a city of over 20 million and still feel alone. She stops crying long enough to buy some fruit and vegetables for her evening meal and walks to the auto rickshaw stand. The words she needs to get home are not coming to her. Again the tears start to fall when behind her she hears a voice: "Aap acha Hindi bol rahee hain." "You are speaking good Hindi." It's her language teacher! Her teacher says in English, "Don't be so hard on yourself!" At this moment, Meri's tears become sobs as she realizes she is no longer alone. Someone sees her pain. Her teacher stands by her at her most vulnerable point.

This is not the last time Meri will cry over Hindi, but she will not feel alone anymore. She knows that Jesus is with her. She knows that she has more than a language teacher; she has a friend who accepts her through tears, frustrations, and all! And she knows she will fight to speak Hindi so that she can fight to save girls like Anu.

BUT NOW THAT FEELING WAS VISCERAL.

DAY FIVE

FROM NA
TO CLOT

This Indian cemetery is not a manicured garden; it's not a place of peace and meditation. Broken tombstones and overgrown, tangled weeds greet them in this British era burial ground. Marble statues of famous military leaders are intact with frozen faces that death cannot destroy. They follow the path to the left. Post-monsoon heat steams from broken bricks as they pick their way toward the gaping hole. Bazaar dogs with ribs poking through sparse bristles of hair growl a threat.

Pastor leads the way. Rohan follows. He carries a wooden box barely the size of a jewelry case. Two gravediggers in dirty lungis lean on their shovels, weary and sweat-soaked. Our group encircles the grave. Rohan bends tenderly, brushing sand and pebbles aside, clearing a resting place for the tiny coffin. I hear Jane's breath catch. Bradley holds her closer. A week before they would've never imagined standing here. None of us could imagine that this hole, instead of her mother's arms, would cradle the beautiful body of their first-born, a daughter. A sudden sickness resulted in a stillborn child, two words that should not go together.

We pray, read a Scripture, and sing. The intensity of the noonday sun is only surpassed by the intensity of Bradley and Jane's agony. Rohan gently sets the wooden box in the deep hole that dwarfs its contents. As the first shovel of dirt hits the top of the coffin, Jane begins to weep, turns, and hides her face against Bradley's shoulder. He quickly draws her toward the path away from the grave. Others follow as sandy dirt and stones continue to rain down on the tiny box. Pastor suggests we move back, out of the way of the two shovels flinging dirt in all directions. "I don't think I can stand this," I murmur to Pastor. "Yes, you can, Beth," he says. "This is what friends do. We wait until it's finished."

Bradley and Jane met three years before in India. A whirlwind courtship closely followed by a multi-national band of friends and overseen by Indian leaders culminated when Bradley knelt in front of the Taj Mahal, world renowned memorial to married love, and slipped a diamond on Jane's left hand. In deference to Indian cultural sensibilities, Bradley's father flew from the U.S. to be there, lending weight and authority to this important occasion. He stood nearby to photograph the engagement.

The wedding was an international celebration. Friends and family from two continents gathered to decorate the wedding hall. The reception was a collaboration of East and West with late night dancing to a mixture of throbbing tabla and Western tunes. Their hearts were settled in India, and they committed to love each other well, to build a life in this urban cultural center, and to form deep relationships that would blossom into a kingdom community. But now this—a storybook wedding marred by death.

And just as in their courtship journey, so now also, Bradley and Jane are closely observed, but this time, naked in their pain. Would they survive? Would they stay in India? Would they run? Of course, there are always negative voices: "If only you'd gone to America, this would never have happened. What were you thinking, trying to have a baby in India?" Those voices fail to recognize that India has the youngest population in the world, and as such, Indian doctors deliver more babies than doctors in any other nation.

Bradley and Jane learned to navigate the crowds and traffic of a megacity. They learned to speak Hindi and to build a business in an Indian setting. They learned to shop and to cook, serve, and entertain in an Indian context. They built close friendships and navigated cultural diversities; they moved easily between Western and Eastern norms. They stopped referring to America as the land of milk and honey, or even home. They loved India. But nothing prepared them for this—raw pain and agony lived naked, not just in front of followers of Jesus, but in open view of those still on the journey, many wondering if Jesus was just another amulet worn around the neck or arm to ward off evil. If that is the case, it certainly did not work this time.

Fifty people attend a memorial service at a friend's apartment—an unexpected gathering in India. Babies born dead are not memorialized. They are quietly disposed of, rarely even held by the mother. Such a child is never buried in a cemetery. Bradley and Jane's desire to celebrate eternal life in the midst of temporal death is a wild stand against Indian cultural norms. We join them in singing "It Is Well With My Soul." We listen as a friend reads Isaiah 55:10–11: "Just as rain and snow descend from the skies and don't go back until they've watered the earth, doing their work of making things grow and blossom, producing seed for farmers and food for the hungry, so will the words that come out of my mouth not come back empty-handed. They'll do the work I sent them to do, they'll complete the assignment I gave them."

Seeds are sown for basically two reasons: food or flowers. Bradley and Jane wonder if the sowing of this very precious seed of their love could possibly do either? In bold brokenness Bradley and Jane tell their friends, "In the last few days, God has shown us once again that through Jesus He promises everlasting life to people filled with pain. If we have seemed strong, it is only because He is good, He is strong, and He is our hope. We believe that God loves us and that He sings His love over our lives—love seen and heard in the many gifts that He gives us."

breaking
bread

R
E
A
D

↳

LUKE 10:25–37

AUTHENTIC
VULNERABILITY

REFLECTION

- In this short story Jesus shows what it means to be a good neighbor. **It is not just helping people we know and love but helping anyone who is vulnerable and in need.** The more we are authentic about our own weaknesses and vulnerabilities the more tender hearted we will be.

- The Jews of that day looked down on Samaritans. They considered them outsiders. Two fellow Jews should have helped but walked by. It was only the Samaritan who stopped and helped. **It would have been easy for him to keep going, worrying what his Samaritan friends would think of him helping a Jew.**

- The good Samaritan not only stopped. He bandaged his wounds, put him on his own donkey, took him to an inn, and paid for all the things he would need. He did not think of the cost to himself; rather, he thought more about the cost of inaction. To not act was to consign this beaten man to death.

- **A good neighbor is always willing to help** those who are vulnerable, no matter where they are from. Even if they think of themselves as our enemies, we are still called to be their neighbors.

As you break the bread and drink the cup together today...

- **Remember today that we were vulnerable enemies of God, and Christ stopped to pick us up.** We are here today because Jesus was a good neighbor to us.

- **Remember there are brothers and sisters in Christ today who are in need.** We are responsible to pick them up.

- **Remember those today who are outside Christ, separated from God by sin.** They are broken, walking the roads of life and looking for answers.

REMEMBRANCE

We covenant today to open our eyes to the hurting and vulnerable around us, remembering that we also have been hurting and vulnerable. We will not pull back, worrying what others might think of us, but we will engage with those who need Jesus. Help us to love, Lord Jesus, the way You love. No more enemies, only friends.

COMMITMENT

We covenant today to open our eyes to the hurting and vulnerable around us. We will not pull back, worrying what others might think of us, but we will engage with those who need Jesus. Help us to love, Lord Jesus, the way You love. No more enemies, only friends.

WEEK 3, DAY 1

An invitation to authenticity.

You've begun inviting others to the table with you. Next, you'll start deepening these relationships by being open and real. Today, take a step toward deepening your authenticity by opening up first to God.

Write a note to God and invite His grace to fill in any inadequacies you may be feeling.

WEEK 3, DAY 2

An invitation to your story.

Usha's story is transforming her village. Part of coming to the table with others is listening and sharing life stories. Today, take a few minutes to write out your life story within the context of the transformation Jesus has done in your life.

Invite someone you are investing in back to the table to share. Listen first to their story and be prepared to share.

WEEK 3, DAY 3

An invitation to turn around.

Being authentic often means we have to turn around and face the very thing we've been running from. Today, get honest about what you have been avoiding.

Write it down and make a plan to face it with God's help. Maybe you need to invite someone to the table for reconciliation.

_____

_____

_____

_____

_____

_____

_____

_____

_____

_____

WEEK 3, DAY 4

An invitation to push through the hard.

Learning a language was hard for Meri. She first had to be able to communicate before she could effectively invite trafficked women to the table with her. Today, be authentic about the breaking points you are experiencing in your life right now.

Who will be most impacted when you experience breakthrough? Remind yourself that for every breaking point, a breakthrough follows.

_____

_____

_____

_____

_____

_____

_____

_____

_____

_____

WEEK 3, DAY 5

An invitation to strength.

Life can be filled with unforeseen circumstances and pain. Today, you have a choice. You can walk through suffering in loneliness or invite God and others in. Together, we discover a divine source of strength and even beauty within life's pain.

Write down some pains you've been experiencing. Commit to bring your suffering to a table with others, and share both with them and God.

_____

_____

_____

_____

_____

_____

_____

_____

_____

_____

_____

_____

_____

_____

_____

_____

_____

_____

_____

_____

_____

_____

_____

_____

_____

_____

_____

_____

_____

_____

beauty within life's pain

week four
family–
community

day

wisdom

In one 24-hour period, flying 8,043 miles across 10 time zones, he misplaced his expertise. It was like lost luggage, out there somewhere, except he didn't know where exactly or when he'd be able to retrieve it. FedEx could not deliver it to his house and the airline insurance policy did not cover the extent of his loss.

In America, Atticus is a respected teacher. His extended family is proud of him, and his community is glad to have a committed family man teaching its high school students. Atticus is not just an expert teacher, though; he is a good husband, father, son, and brother. He knows what is expected of him, and he knows how to get things done. He knows which government offices can help him with certain issues. He knows his way around and where the necessary stores are: Home Depot, Kinkos, the post office, Outback Steakhouse, and Applebees. That abruptly changed when he moved to India.

Atticus stopped looking for his expertise when he discovered the amazing wisdom of his Indian family-community *(these words are hyphenated because India hyphenates them).* And as he owns up to what he does not know, India becomes his teacher, because to be found in India is to be welcomed, wanted, desired, sheltered, taken in, pulled close, and never let go.

India teaches him that "the guest is god." If he drops in on someone, it's not awkward, and people never feel inconvenienced. He is never an interruption. In fact, Indians are proud to have him in their home, and he knows the worst thing he can say to his hostess is, "Don't go to any trouble to make chai." They bring a basin and pitcher and pour water over his hands so that he can eat with his fingers. They serve him and then stand and watch as each bite goes into his mouth—the joy they show at his enjoyment! India has definitely tutored Atticus in art of the welcome.

India also teaches him that acquaintances are family, and they have zero anxiety over physical contact. His wife Kate visits an acquaintance and finds they already view her as family. They invite her to pile up on the bed with the women, talking, laughing, and eating. Atticus himself was not ready for much manly contact, but he understands now that when a guy shakes his hand and then continues to hold it or puts his arm around Atticus's shoulder as they walk down the road, he is in their inner circle. This is a safe place, and the smartest thought Atticus has at that moment is, "Well, we're going to snuggle, I guess." India tutors him in the art of affectionate, family-community physical contact.

India teaches him that relationships start small but quickly grow wide. What appears to be a random cup of tea with a security guard can easily progress to a one and a half hour train trip to the man's home and the honor of being the first white person in this Muslim village and the first to be served sweets by his mother in their family home. In the process, everyone who knows and accepts the security guard will know and accept Atticus, and by the time he's ready to leave the village and travel back home, Atticus has ten more invitations to visit in ten different homes. India has tutored him in the art of inclusion.

India teaches him that asking personal questions shows a desire for relationship. Now when he hears, "what did you eat today," he knows that means, "I'd love to teach you how to make Bengali lentils; we could do it together and then eat together." The astonished question "do you eat with your fingers" means "you don't think you're better than me; you're just like me!" Or "who's your prophet" means "my religion is woven into every fiber of my life and I'm not ashamed or afraid to talk about it." Then there's "you don't know where to buy a hammer and nails" means "I'll stop everything I'm doing to go with you so you won't be taken advantage of." What's your name? What's your home country? What's your religion? Do you eat beef? Can we be friends on Facebook? These are no longer intrusive questions to Atticus. India has tutored him in the art of candor, kindness, and cooperation.

"I never would have made it this far without the wisdom and common sense of my Indian family-community," says Atticus. "When the electrician comes to fix something, he ends up on the floor playing with my kids, and we invite him to eat lunch with us, we make a friend forever." When a village woman, holding Kate and Atticus's 7-month-old son, says, "What's wrong with his head? It isn't shaped right," they are not offended. Instead, they visit the doctor who sends them to a specialist who sends them to America for a life-saving operation. The boy is fine, and the family is fine. They know they owe that woman the life of their son. When they invite a large group of their village friends to their home for Thanksgiving, they start a tradition of reading from the Injil Sharif *(New Testament)* and saying what they're thankful for. Everyone says, "We're thankful for you. You're just like family." They know those words would not be said and a number of young men would not decide to follow Jesus if Atticus and Kate did not let India teach them about family-community.

"LIVE LIKE JESUS DID AND THE WORLD WILL LISTEN."

- Mahatma Gandhi

PROTECTION

The winter sun slips below the horizon, but there is still enough light for Cristina to walk the path without a flashlight. She's on her way home from the café where she teaches music and dance, connecting and building relationships that will impact eternity. A friend gives her a ride on a scooter and drops her at the ATM near her house. She needs to withdraw money for rent, but as is common in this town the machine is empty. She'll try again tomorrow. She notices a security guard in the ATM's back room; a second man is there as well. Cristina recognizes him as a person who has followed her a few times. She pushes the thought aside, "I'm just being paranoid."

This is a particularly safe Indian town, especially now that winter's chill is in the air. The area is inundated with tourists from Delhi and the Punjab in the summer months, and that's when girls cautiously walk alone in public. Groups of young men accustomed to the free, easy lifestyle of large cities can be annoying, even aggressive. But as the winter snow moves toward this northern town, the streets become still and empty. Local residents are conservative and family centered. Any man who attempts to misbehave with a woman will be dealt with severely, and everyone knows it.

Cristina pulls her debit card from the machine, slips it in her backpack, and begins to walk home. This has been a life-changing year for her. She graduated from college, moved from Connecticut to India, began studying Hindi, and discovered that the abilities God nurtured in her are strategic gifts to build friendships. She's from a close-knit Puerto Rican family, so community is foundational to her life. Still, India is teaching her a new depth of community, and she's grateful that Jesus led her here.

She passes four small open-air restaurants. Sandwich board signs list the simple menu: ginger-lemon-honey-tea, bun-omelet, and paratha. Even on this chilly winter evening, they're open, with tables and chairs out front. The occasional car slowly maneuvers around the tables that sit on the road's edge. The occasional mule walks by, the bell around its neck clanging as it meanders up the road looking for grass on the way home. A shop owner waves in recognition and greeting as he snaps on the outdoor lights. Cristina stops here often. She meets friends around these tables and even enjoys chai with the owner's daughter. She waves back and continues walking.

Cristina hears someone on the road behind her but at first thinks nothing of it. The majority of residents don't own cars, so walking is common. It's not until she nears the deserted road leading to her house that she senses something wrong. She glances back and recognizes the man from the ATM. She takes out her phone, and though she's out of minutes, fakes a phone call. Walking more slowly, she pretends to talk to someone and allows the man to pass her. But suddenly he turns, asks a question in Hindi, and advances threateningly toward her. "You'd better move away or I'll call my uncle," Cristina says to him. Adults are often referred to in relationship terms in India, even if not related by blood. Cristina is confident in her own strength; after all she does CrossFit and is a dancer. He doesn't move away. He grabs her and pins her against the stonewall as he tears at her clothes.

SHE KICKS WI
FRIGHTENED,
THAT HE IS ST

She kicks wildly, frightened, aware that he is stronger. She screams. The man knows his community and realizes the screams of a young woman will not go unnoticed. He lets go and runs back the direction from which he came. Shaken, Cristina sprints for home.

What happens next and in the months to come solidify Christina's confidence in the power of a protecting community. Shortly after the incident, her leaders John and Ann comfort and question her. They then walk back with her to confront the man. John opens the ATM door, makes eye contact with the guy, then puts him up against the wall, yelling at him in Hindi, shaming him for his actions. Only steps away from the sidewalk cafe, the owners come out as John tells them about what's just happened to Cristina. She is surprised, even overwhelmed, by the shopkeepers' reactions, the tenderness and care with which they comfort her. They then take over where John left off, angrily addressing the man, telling him he's a shame to their community and should move to Delhi because he's not wanted here any longer.

Since then, the shopkeepers are truly Cristina's "uncles." They treat her as their own daughters and offer to have someone walk with her whenever she passes. Word travels fast in India, and the story of her assault filters through the bazaar. A Muslim tailor informs her that he heard and invites her to have chai with his three daughters. He assures her that she is a true member of their family and they're always ready to help. This opens the door for more visits and a growing relationship with the eldest daughter. Other acquaintances she meets at the café tell her she's now not only a friend but family as well. "As crazy as it all was, all of my relationships grew deeper because of that week," Cristina says. "I know without a doubt that if I'm ever in trouble, my community will protect of me."

DAY 3

care & concern

She walks fast as she sobs uncontrollably. She dials her team leader on the cell phone. Her team leader can't understand the garbled sentences so she waits patiently as Katrina composes herself.

"He came and got Rebecca," she was finally able to say.

"Who came and got Rebecca? Is she alright? Where is she?"

"She's alright. She's home now with Sataswari."

Rufus and Katrina, and their 2-year-old son and 1-year-old daughter arrived in India six months before. It is the fulfillment of Katrina's lifelong dream. From the time she was a little girl, all she wanted to be was a missionary. Rufus spent a year abroad right after college. There was no going back; he was settled in his calling. India was to be their family's exciting and at times disturbing adventure— exciting for Rufus and disturbing for Katrina.

They moved to a neighborhood and had team members in the same building. It comforted Katrina to know that her kids had an auntie right downstairs, and she had a prayer partner. She met once a week with a group of women, both Americans and Indians to worship and pray together. Katrina learned to open her life to her Indian sisters and shared her fears and concerns. They were kind and caring, praying strength and peace into her. Throughout, Katrina found a new joy in prayer. She was frequently told that she had the gift of intercession, and Jesus used that gift to help her empathize with and intercede for her newfound family.

Their team leader often encouraged Katrina and Rufus that in every relationship with followers of Jesus, they build a community of grace. She said that those outside the community would be drawn to their love and care for each other, and it was very possible outsiders would belong before they believe. They heard stories of persecution when someone from a Hindu, Muslim, or Buddhist background declared their faith in Jesus, and they learned that Indian family-community is very strong and a decision to go against the norm could be a decision to be ostracized, disowned, beaten, or jailed. Katrina and Rufus were committed to show the love of Jesus and to welcome those who weren't His followers into their circle of life.

Katrina and Rufus soon became friends with their neighbors. The father, Rajnish, is a young man, a Hindu, and a political leader in the area. He was always willing to help. Rufus asked, "Where do I go to get a new lock? How can I fix my refrigerator? Is there a way to get faster Internet? What's causing that bad sewage smell in our house?" Always Rajnish spent hours helping Rufus solve the problem, and they were grateful for his help. But soon Katrina became uncomfortable. She knew they passed the test of being open and drawing Rajnish and his family into their lives. His children were regular playmates for their children. His wife, though shy, invited Katrina for tea or stopped by for a visit. Rajnish felt more and more comfortable just walking into their house.

And then it happens. Katrina and Rufus are at language school. Their son Christopher is at pre-school, and their daughter Rebecca is home with their house helper, Sataswari, a gentle follower of Jesus. Rebecca starts to cry, and Sataswari cannot calm her. Rajnish, the helpful neighbor, hears Rebecca crying, walks into the house, scolds Sataswari, and walks out the door with the baby. Sataswari calls Katrina immediately, and Katrina quickly goes home. Rebecca is fine. Rajnish is distracting her outside to help her stop crying. He will do anything to placate her, believing he is doing what is best for her and being a good friend to the family in the process. Katrina is distraught, though. What are the boundaries between living an open life for the sake of the gospel and protecting her child?

There is a host of things that Rufus and Katrina learned through this episode. She knows that the whole family-community cares for the Indian children, although there is never a question about who the parents are, so she starts to step out on the tight rope to learn the balance between her absolute commitment to Rebecca and Christopher and her absolute commitment to Jesus' command to love her neighbor. She also learns her responsibility to teach Sataswari to obey their directions when it comes to their children. As a follower of Jesus, Sataswari needs to learn to be under their authority as she works for them, and Rufus and Katrina see the reminders that God places authorities in their lives to guide and protect them. Rufus learns that he can discuss concerns with Rajnish, and when they don't respond in anger, a friendship is strengthened and a relationship is not thrown away. They experience the power of community with other followers of Jesus who they can call at a moment's notice, and they see an inter-connected community way of life that cuts across the American independent way of life. Most of all, they see the grace that Jesus gives them to trust their family to Him.

DAY FOUR

OPEN DO

He always thought that to entertain his family needed a decent dining room table. "I could never extend an invitation if I didn't have the right stuff in my house." But now Doug realizes how limited that perspective is and discovers it's not furniture standing in his way, it's his pride. He cares more about what people think of him and his possessions, than caring about them. Here in India, people with no table at all invite him to eat at their house. They sit on the bed or on a mat on the floor if there's enough floor space. Hospitality has no required equipment.

The Muslim village that is Doug and his wife Carrie's community is a suburb on the southern edge of a megacity of over 20 million people. That's the population of New York City, Los Angeles, Chicago, Houston, and Philadelphia combined. Most people in this Indian city have never had an opportunity to know a Jesus-follower because there are simply not enough to go around. And there never will be if we don't walk through people's doors, and into their houses, kitchens, and lives—and if we don't invite them into ours.

Doug and his family quickly learned that there's no set time for hospitality. For their first invitation to a home, they have no idea what to expect. Their hosts say, "Come in the evening," so they arrive at 6 thinking they will eat and leave by 7:30, or 8 at the latest. But the hostess plans to get her ingredients from the bazaar at 8. So Carrie joins the ladies in the kitchen where they hand her a bowl of chapatti dough and she rolls her first unleavened whole wheat bread. The chapattis turn out more square than round, but everyone laughs and no one seems to mind. From that day on, Carrie heads straight to the kitchen whenever the family receives an invitation for a meal—not to hurry the proceedings along, but to spend every possible minute learning hospitality. Now her repertoire of Indian food is pretty expansive. More than that, her friend group is expansive, and each friend opens doors for more friendships.

Fish opens doors in their community. One day, Doug joins a group of men from his village for some fishing and catches the biggest fish of the day. His friends are ecstatic and congratulate him on his accomplishment and then brag about him to everyone who will listen. After a bit, he finally works up the courage to say, "I don't know what to do with the fish. I don't know how to clean it." His friends walk him to their house where they cut and clean the fish and return it to him. Another day, Carrie is eating some fish curry and although she is using her fingers, she finds it still difficult to navigate the bones. Fatima sees her struggling, so she reaches over, takes Carrie's plate, and proceeds to de-bone it with her fingers. She

smashes it to make sure there are no bones that will get caught in her throat and returns the plate. At first Carrie is grossed out; every bit of her food was just manhandled by fingers other than her own. But she realizes what an act of kindness Fatima has exhibited.

Carrie's willingness to eat food right from that woman's fingers opened doors of relationship for the family. Children, until they are 5 or 6, eat rice and dal mixed together and served by someone's fingers—and it's rarely the mother's fingers. It may be

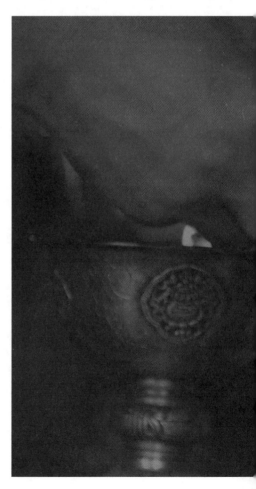

an older sibling, aunt, grandma, or neighbor. Every birthday cake is cut by the one celebrating, and the first piece is fed into the mouth of an honored guest. At weddings, guests walk up to the bride and groom, pick up a round, white roshagulla or a piece of sandesh and feed the wedding couple. Then they finish it off by lifting a glass of milk to wash down the sweet. Feeding someone is an act of loving hospitality, and the willingness to be fed an act of accepting hospitality.

hospitality

day

Kingdom

of Community

There was no exposure to TV preachers or American churches. This was the first time the world saw a transformational Jesus community in action. God tore the curtain that separated Him from humanity. Jesus died to restore that relationship. As the Kingdom comes on earth, the first relationship restored is man's relationship to God. The next restoration is man's relationship to man.

Acts 2 tells the powerful story. The setting is not that different from daily life in an Indian bazaar: an ancient religious worship center built of hand-hewn stone, crowds of people pushing and shoving into the same small space, loud noises permeating every corner of the building, a thousand voices speaking simultaneously in a thousand languages. What is different from our Indian bazaar is the wildfire of the Holy Spirit that spreads through their ranks. Peter's voice clearly proclaims the life, death, and resurrection of Jesus and the formation of a radical community.

"There's no longer room for doubt—God made him Master and Messiah, this Jesus whom you killed on a cross." Cut to the quick, those who were listening asked Peter and the other apostles, "Brothers! Brothers! So now what do we do?" Peter said, "Change your life. Turn to God and be baptized, each of you in the name of Jesus Christ, so your sins are forgiven. Receive the gift of the Holy Spirit. The promise is targeted to you and your children, but also to all who are far away—whomever, in fact, our Master God invites" *(Acts 2:36–39).*

Before we know it "all the believers lived in a wonderful harmony, holding everything in common. They sold whatever they owned and pooled their resources so that each person's need was met. They followed a daily discipline of worship in the Temple followed by meals at home, every meal a celebration, exuberant and joyful, as they praised God. Every day their number grew as God added those who were saved" *(vv. 44–47).*

How do we get from our restoration to God and receiving the gift of the Holy Spirit to this kind of radical community fleshed out in real people's lives? We recognize that neither American nor Indian community is the Scriptural ideal. That neither Western nor Eastern culture can fully reveal God's Kingdom.

First, we have to broaden our definition of family. Radical community of restored relationships is the Kingdom here. In America, "me" includes me, my wife, and my kids. In India "me" includes me, my wife, my kids, my parents, my in-laws, my brothers and sisters, and their spouses and kids. In God's Kingdom, everyone is my family; everyone is my responsibility.

We learn to be this together. We share houses, cars, meals, prayer, coffee, hospital bills, tools, blankets, chocolate chips, water, computers, washing machines and dryers, books, pots and pans, scooters, electricity, refrigerators, stoves, and money. Many of us live without personal transportation, and even if we have a car or scooter with our name on it, we make it available to others. We notice that cars with windows rolled up insulate us from our neighbors, so we walk more. That makes it easier to stop for a visit and a cup of tea. We commit to use public transportation so that we're sitting next to real Indian people and can have real conversations. Some of us intentionally walk on city streets every day, praying, observing, so that we remember what the real world is like for those who live in desperate poverty on our streets.

We choose to live lives of giving and receiving. Some of our American team members have committed to live on the salary of a middle-class Indian, learning to spend finances differently than what was their habit in American. Some give away twice as much as they spend on themselves, others put a new roof on a neighbor's house before they roof their own house. Some spend what they would save for retirement when there's a need in the community. Others chose to not buy a house in America so that their hearts will be settled in India.

We're learning that institutional compassion will never meet the needs of the world. We want to be generous with more than stuff. We're choosing to be generous with our lives. That kind of generosity can't be lived by dropping cans off at a soup kitchen, no matter how helpful that is. This is the invite people home, cook them a meal and listen to their story kind of generosity. And it can be uncomfortable and expensive.

We choose to commit to daily teaching and prayer. Every single day we study the Word of God together. Every single day we spend extended time praying together. Every single day we're sitting at a common table, sharing food, building family. Every single day we challenge our community of Jesus followers to reproduce Jesus life. We're not going to hand people a book to read. We want them to read our lives. We're not going to tell them to go to church or go to a conference or go to a concert. We choose instead to say, "come and see." We choose to live Matthew 5:16

"Keep open house; be generous with your lives. By opening up to others, you'll prompt people to open up with God, this generous Father in heaven."

We're learning to love the diversity of people God has created and placed in our lives. And that's more than just the Jesus followers. We rejoice in the variety of skin colors, the cacophony of languages and the intricate cultures of the peoples of India. They are our love because God loves them. We rejoice in them because God rejoices in them. We give ourselves to be family to them because we've been drawn into God's family. We invite them into our lives because we are people who've accepted God's invitation. We figure that if Jesus sent us to India it's because he's planning to show up here. And we want him to show up in our friendships and relationships.

We're still figuring out how to live this kind of radical community. We still make mistakes. We still fight our insecurities, insensitivities and selfishness. But we're committed. We're looking for others who will commit to this common table way of life with us.

breaking
bread

R
E
A
D
↳

EPHESIANS 2:11–22

RECOGNIZING
COMMUNITY

REFLECTION

- **Sin not only separated us from God; it separated us from one another.** Jesus came to tear down the walls of separation, so that we might walk with God and with one another.

- **Jesus is daily building us up** as a people to reveal His glory to the nations.

- **We are able to sit together** at a table set by God today because of what Christ did for us.

REMEMBRANCE

As you break the bread and drink the cup together today...

- **Remember that it is only through the death of Christ** that we have been brought near to God. He paid the price for my sin.

- **Remember that not only have we become right with God,** but we can also be in right relationship with one another.

- **Remember those today who are not at the table,** those who do not know that a way has been made for eternal life.

COMMITMENT

I covenant today to live in right relationship with Jesus and with all people. I covenant to treat every fellow disciple as a part of my family. I covenant to use every opportunity I have to let those on the outside know there is place already set for them at the table.

WEEK 4, DAY 1

An invitation to family.

God's definition of family often times surpasses ours. What does it mean to you to open your life to a new definition of family?

Write today how your life would look differently if you opened it up to strangers and became more like brothers, sisters, aunts, and uncles.

_____

_____

_____

_____

_____

_____

_____

_____

_____

_____

_____

_____

WEEK 4, DAY 2

An invitation to purpose-filled risk.

Living life among community and re-defining family can be risky. While it is wise to protect yourself in many circumstances, protection can also become a barrier to relationships.

What are some barriers you've created in your life that can be safely taken down within the context of a supportive community?

_____

_____

_____

_____

_____

_____

_____

_____

_____

_____

WEEK 4, DAY 3

An invitation to trust.

As we invite people into our lives, it can be scary. It takes a supernatural dependance on God. He can give us discernment and wisdom as to how to relate and when to trust new family members.

Ask yourself today, am I prepared to build more trusting relationships with others? What would that look like in your day-to-day life?

_____
_____
_____
_____
_____
_____
_____
_____
_____
_____
_____
_____

WEEK 4, DAY 4

An invitation to extravagant hospitality.

Often in today's culture, we allow someone to serve us when we go out to eat versus us inviting others into our home environment and serving them. Today, set a date with a person in whom you are investing to have them to your home. Prepare your home to serve your best and, once you do, come back to this page and write down how it felt to be a giver of extravagant hospitality.

What did you learn about yourself?

_____
_____
_____
_____
_____
_____
_____
_____
_____
_____

WEEK 4, DAY 5

An invitation to share.

In India, sharing is a way of life similar to the model in the book of Acts. Ask yourself today, what are a few things that I would never consider sharing? Choose one of those things this week to give up for someone else's benefit. If you can't think of anything, try the reverse question: "Is there anything a 'brother or sister' is needing that I have?"

Make the decision to sacrificially give.

Share
what
you
won't

week five

the joy choice

day one

choose expectation

"Come on. I want to show you something." He starts down the dirt path, manhandling a rusty lock on the metal gate. Tom puts his shoulder against it and finally slams it with his foot to get it open. I ask about the long, low stone building to their right—the walls still intact, the roof caved in. The former owner of this property, a man from Afghanistan, built it and lived there. That made sense. I could easily imagine that building on a craggy mountain in Afghanistan: half house, half fortress.

"We've got a water problem," Tom says, "and it's one that the government won't be fixing anytime soon. I've wanted to bore a well, but apparently, it takes lots of application forms and a significant bribe to get permission to bring in that heavy equipment. A local landlord and friend suggested I do it the old-fashioned way." Fifty chickens clucked in a small enclosure. "Yeah, we decided to raise chickens, and now we're planting vegetables. It's part of taking care of the earth. Part of living sustainably."

This 6'1" American often surprises me. He looks like he would be right at home in the hallowed halls of Harvard or UC Berkley. His education and reading list are impressive. I've heard him hold the attention of a room as he shares his Indian journey: early excitement, adrenaline pumping, traveling the continent with his young bride, two children born in quick succession, overwhelming problems, health issues, isolation, disillusionment, discouragement. They were ready to walk away from India—this land that takes your breath away and then quite literally, can take your breath away.

But this family made some strategic decisions. Those decisions didn't necessarily make life any easier—just more harmonious, as he says.

- *They would do whatever God told them to do.*

- *They would make close Indian friendships.*

- *They would take care of their family.*

In that order.

I step carefully to avoid some prickly cactus as I watch how a nearby healthy black bull will react to our presence. He ignores us, intent on filling his belly while stopping intermittently to bellow. That's when I see "the old-fashioned way": three skinny guys in threadbare lungis, pulled up and tucked between their legs into makeshift shorts, a hole dug with shovels and a pick-axe, and bucketfuls of dirt and rocks hauled up and dumped around the parameter. It is not very impressive, but there is some water in the bottom of the hole now. That looks promising.

When choosing your favorite flavored mineral water or putting your BPA-free bottle under the spout on your refrigerator door with the decision of crushed ice or cubes, digging a well to get a drink seems like something people do in another galaxy, definitely another century.

Jesus said we would be rewarded even if we only gave someone a drink of water in His name. In many places of the world, that seems like a reward that isn't earned. But someone had the vision for that reservoir, water treatment plant, miles of pipe, and a faucet. Someone had the expectation, the faith to lay down their life and do the hard stuff, so that a well of spiritual water could be dug among an unreached people group in India.

And it isn't the bottle, the glass, or the crystal goblet that makes the drink valuable. It's a friend who understands you well enough to notice when you're thirsty, who knows where and how to get a drink, and who then actually brings it to you. That's worth a lot.

BUT THIS FAMILY MADE SOME STRATEGIC DECISIONS.

DAY TWO

CHOOSE
ENDURA

If Dennis was in charge, there would be only one color in the rainbow: orange. On the soccer field, he's hard to miss. He's the guy in the bright orange jersey and big smile, and when he opens his mouth out comes a European accent. He was a white-blond, 3-year-old, Dutch kid on the streets of Curacao *(a Dutch island in the Caribbean)* when he kicked his first football, okay, soccer ball—and he never stopped. Soccer is his love and his gift, but it's only recently that he discovered a deep calling to use that gift to reach the unreached.

Dennis grew up like so many children in the Netherlands, eating dinner while watching soccer on TV, and he still sneaks out of bed at 1 a.m. to watch a big match. In Europe, if you're good enough at the game at the age of 12, you're encouraged to go for it. Dennis was good, and though his dad was an enthusiastic Dutch football fan, he definitely didn't see it as a viable future for his son. He was from a family of successful entrepreneurs, and he saw the drive and endurance in Dennis and wanted to channel that drive toward business.

But Dennis had other plans. At 16, he sold his scooter and moved to the U.S. An American soccer coach traveling in Europe saw him play and offered him a job at a soccer camp in Tennessee. He went on to play college soccer where he met his wife, Mia. Dennis thought when he came to America, he could get away from his father and do the one thing he loved: play football. But God had other plans. For the first time in his life, Dennis was introduced to Jesus. Mia and Dennis married and very quickly had a daughter. The pressures of family life and financial responsibility forced him into the business world where he thrived. But the love for football never left him—the thrill of putting on his cleats, pulling his orange jersey over his head, and going for the goal.

As Dennis was learning to walk with Jesus in the business world, he heard a missionary speak about India and the need, the challenge, and the seeming impossibilities of 1.3 billion people, 2,000 unreached people groups, 150 commonly spoken languages, and 1,652 language dialects. India alone has more unreached people groups than the next ten unreached nations combined. Add to that, six megacities with populations over ten million each. "I've never been able to stay away from a challenge," Dennis says. "I quit my job, sold our house, took Mia, and moved our family of four children to India. I didn't have a clue that God was setting me up for the biggest game of my life. This was going to take much more skill and endurance than I ever imagined."

During the first few years he established a football club that drew hundreds of avid players. His business experienced a hostile takeover. Competitors, jealous of his success, came after him, tried to get him thrown out of India. Earlier injuries caused Dennis longstanding challenges. He contracted dengue fever; one son had an emergency appendectomy; another struggled in school; and his house was broken into and they were robbed. The climate was inhospitable, the language difficult, and the business environment intolerable. This was a lot harder than the most difficult match he'd ever played, but God built Dennis for just such a challenge. He learned to spiritually endure at a level he'd never known before. He leaned into Jesus, learned that the Holy Spirit was his strength, listened to his leaders, spent time alone with Jesus, and began to see the game plan God laid out before him.

Today, he leads a sports management company that's impacting India. He says, "Before I would have been too concerned about logistics. Now I'm looking at the end goal: how to use sports to build Jesus communities." And it's happening. A young Bengali boy named Sourav arrived with his suitcase. He was a lasi wallah; he made buttermilk drinks on a street corner. He was desperate for a shot. He now lives with a group of footballers that are being discipled and playing soccer. Another young man, Rohit, heard about the program and traveled over 1,200 miles to join. He's not a very good player, but he's been drawn into the life of the club. Other players are coming from Muslim nations in Africa, and they are all challenged with the goals of discipline, commitment, character, and integrity.

"I haven't been so excited in years," Dennis says. "I love doing football, but I really love doing what Jesus made me for. I'm not perfect, but I feel like I'm pleasing Jesus using football to disciple Jesus followers."

day three

choose correction

She's an introvert. Anyone in her family can tell you that, and her few close friends will attest to it. All the personality tests she's taken verify the truth.

Joy gave up all her American rights to come to India, so she figured it was OK to hang on to a couple of her "things": her introvert nature, her early bedtime, and her alone time. She decided she could be little picky about food, too: no MSG, nothing oily, nothing too spicy, and no Indian sweets. This was who she was—take it or leave it. She knew she didn't really need many friends, and she really had no desire to hang out with large groups of people.

But she did sense that God called her to India, an extremely relational country with a massive population.

Joy was well into her second year living in one of India's megacities before she began to hear the truth: everyone thought she was a jerk. They called her a "waster" because she constantly turned down invitations. In India, if someone refuses an invitation a couple times, the group just leaves that person alone. They figure that person doesn't like them and doesn't want to be around them. Indians won't force themselves on anyone.

Joy made this discovery because Ranbir was brave enough to tell her. He was a humorous guy that teased her in a funny way, until she finally grew tired of being teased. That's when the Holy Spirit spoke to her. The conviction was strong and uncomfortable and corroborated everything that Ranbir said. The Spirit said: "Either you can eat the way you want and sleep when you want, or you can have community. It's one or the other. You can make a choice."

She realized she could either hold onto the few things that she says about herself or she could let go and learn to make people her priority. After all, that's what Jesus did. She came to India saying she wanted to be like Jesus and wanted people to see the life of Jesus in her. Here was her opportunity, but it would take listening to the correction of an Indian brother and yielding herself to the transforming work of the Holy Spirit.

COMMUNITY

Joy's life changed for the better because she chose the joy of correction. She worries a lot less now because she sees that she doesn't have to control things as much. She truly feels less need to be in control. She feels less stress when she finds herself waiting for people, and she is learning patience. Now, she eats almost everything, which widens the possibilities of the places she can go and the diverse people she can spend time with.

TRANSFORMING

PATIENCE

Joy now recognizes her need for community. She hungers for food and for people. This is not co-dependency but definitely interdependency. And when she doesn't go out, people now understand

HUNGERS

because she opened herself enough to them to help them understand. How her behavior makes people feel matters more to her now as she wants them to experience the love and inclusion of the Jesus way of life. Being so independent she didn't think of herself as connected to people, but now she appreciates the connections. She actually knows what people think and that began after she became willing to be with them. Joy simply can't tune them out anymore.

She realizes this isn't a cultural difference between

OPENNESS

Americans and Indians. This openness to people and desire to be with them, this kind of community, has a spiritual base. This is her willingness to lay down her life for the sake of building relationship. It's important to be with people because that's real. It's real life.

CHOOSE SACRIFICE

"I want to know if you'll give me some of your life?" I feel like I'm yelling. The restaurant is noisy, packed with young, middle class Indians. It's a Friday night. We are sitting in Chili's, the brand new American addition to this upscale mall in our megacity.

A group of Sikhs with brightly colored turbans arrives laughing and talking. They sit at a table across the aisle from three couples dressed in designer blue jeans, all of whom have the kalava, a braided crimson string, on their wrist, the guys on their right wrist, the gals on their left. The string signifies they participated in a Hindu puja ceremony. Glancing around I notice Ayesha and Rafique who just walked through the door and are waiting for a table. Rafique is an intellectual property lawyer, and Ayesha, a writer. They wave and I walk over to give them a hug and inquire about Rafique's parents. They live together in a Muslim joint-family and had been my neighbors.

"I want to know if you'll give me some of your life?" The question still hung in the air as I return to the table. I'm eating dinner with Sneha and Akshay, and I ask them this strange question in obedience to the Holy Spirit. This young couple has been in my circle of influence for a few years, and although I'd moved from their city, the Lord reconnected us when Akshay's mom died. Akshay is a freelance photographer. Sneha just recently quit her administrative position, but already has leads on some well-paying jobs. "How much of my life do you want?" Akshay replied. "What do you think about two weeks?" I reply. "We'll work out the timing, and I'll send you a ticket."

Seven months and multiple confirmations later, Akshay and Sneha, now pregnant with their first child, resign their jobs and move to a far corner of India, away from their family, their vibrant church community, and lifelong friendships. They move to a place where their mother tongue is not spoken and out of a joint-family home. They leave behind their motorcycle, arrive with four suitcases, and move into a tiny space with a mattress on the floor, no living room furniture, and no refrigerator. They do it to follow God's call on their lives to join a multi-national Live Dead team and plant a Christ-community among the unreached.

Their plan is to return home for the baby's birth, stay a couple months, and return to rejoin their team, but two months later Sneha isn't feeling well. They walk a half-mile to the local hospital and are told that her blood pressure is 180/120. She is nearly ready to go into seizures and needs to be immediately transported forty-five minutes to a larger hospital.

We pray in the Spirit all the way down the winding mountain road. The ob-gyn says that they will work to stabilize her blood pressure and then take the baby by C-section. The problem is the baby is only thirty weeks old and weighs around two pounds. Forty-eight hours later, Sneha is wheeled to the operating room as the chief medical officer, neonatologist, and ob-gyn call Akshay into an office. "We want to be absolutely sure that you understand the risk. We give your baby less than ten percent chance of surviving the delivery. This is a very dangerous situation for your wife as well." He signs the paper saying he understands. We wait and pray, impatient to hear any news. "The baby boy is in the NICU. He's on a ventilator." That morning the Lord woke me with a message for Akshay, "We need to get ready. This is a marathon, not a sprint."

Now hour after hour and day after day, we wait and pray. Sneha's hospital room becomes a revolving door of team members and extended community: the ones we live the life of Jesus before and the ones who have the Kingdom in their eyes but have yet not put their faith in Jesus.

One of the most frequent visitors is Daya. Two days before the emergency trip down the mountain, Daya was walking with Travis. He stopped suddenly, turned, and said, "I'm a follower of Jesus." It had been a two-year process in his life. He joined the CrossFit gym and spent extended hours with Jesus-followers. He was like Nicodemus in John 3, coming to Jesus in the middle of the night. Daya would say things like, "I had a revelation that the universe is good. Something woke me up at 3 a.m. and

I felt the presence of Jesus." Daya was a searcher, a seeker with tough questions, and he struggled with deep insecurities until one day Travis said to him, "Dude, we're all punks if we're not pointing you to Jesus. We can't be the answer to your life. Only He can be."

Now Daya has made his declaration of faith, and the hospital room becomes a spiritual incubator for him with hours of deep discussion and prayer. He watches Sneha and Akshay's faith in action. He sees firsthand that Jesus is the answer for their lives, and it begins to strengthen him in his own new life.

"TRUE LOVE IS SELFLESS. IT IS PREPARED TO SACRIFICE."

- Sadhu Vaswani

DAY 5

choose
salvation

One hundred twenty people make for an enormous dinner party. An enormous dinner party requires an enormous menu: 24 pounds of turkey *(flown from America with friends)*, 66 pounds of halal chicken tandoori, momos *(steamed dumplings)*, chow mein, sweet potatoes, mashed potatoes, cranberries, paneer tikka, rice, four vegetable dishes, rolls, pies, pudding, cookies, kheer *(Indian rice pudding)*, spiced walnut cake, and other eggless and sugar-free dessert choices. And don't forget the drinks: cocoa, coffee, tea, hot apple cider, juices, water, and soda.

The food preparation began days in advance, weeks if you count asking friends to bring turkeys from America. Two mountain men walked for three hours from the backside of the mountain to deliver the huge burlap bags of wood and dried pinecones we bought for a bonfire and grill. There is no Walmart within driving distance in case we run low on fuel for the barbeque. A 30-gallon barrel, cut down the middle and laid on its side, is set up in the backyard for the grill space. Raju and Sonu are the barbeque experts. We string hundreds of lights outside and inside the house. The space is bright and festive. It's as if the almost thirty annual Hindu holidays, random Muslim Eids, and Christmas have been lumped together. And this is just Thanksgiving.

And we are thankful. There are three times as many Indians as there are Americans at the party, and the majority of our guests are not Jesus followers. They are committed Hindus, Muslims, Sikhs, and Buddhists. There are some with cultural loyalty to a religion but who don't observe the religious traditions; they're pretty much secular.

At four o'clock in the afternoon our guests start to arrive. Many are friends we met in our CrossFit gym, and others are regulars at our coffee shop or acquaintances from town. Some had never been to this house; others sat at our table often. They are the ones who walk into the kitchen and lift lids off the pans to look and sniff. There are some who come as friends of friends of friends. "No, it's OK. Just come. They love to feed people."

The work of setting a table that everyone can come to can be extremely challenging. Our Thanksgiving table spans three rooms, and the line goes out the they love to feed people

door. One of the most divisive hours in India is mealtime. We designate vegetarian and non-vegetarian tables, and non-halal dishes are clearly marked. There are as many varieties in food observance here as there are religions.

India is nations within a nation. Most of the twenty-nine states and seven union territories have their own language and culture, and twenty-one of India's states have a population of over six million people. And 10 states each have more than 60 million people. The most populated is home to almost 200 million people. India is also home to five of the world's major religions: Hinduism, Islam, Sikhism, Buddhism, and Jainism.

As followers of Jesus, we don't always do diversity well, and things become a lot harder when we want to open our arms to many different people and invite them to a common table. The more inclusive we are, the harder hospitality is. And we have a tendency to want it easy. The unchallenged moments in life are the easiest. When we act exclusively, life is easier because it's just us in our own homogenous bubble. There is no need to consider what food we serve or what words we say or how we act. There is no need to care about people. Not only do we not want to lay our lives down for people who we don't love or who are different from us, but we definitely won't inconvenience ourselves for them.

But our gospel is an inconvenient gospel. It was inconvenient for Jesus, and it will be inconvenient for us. Two thousand years after He died and was resurrected, nearly half the world still has not heard about Him because we decided we don't want to be inconvenienced. The nation of India, these nations within a nation, by population and unreached peoples is one-third of the Great Commission. Our selfishness and self-centeredness are our greatest challenges to setting a table that welcomes the world to know the Savior of the world.

At our multi-national, multi-ethnic Thanksgiving, we eat for hours and play word games, volleyball, and soccer. Deep life-changing conversation and laughter flow across the fields and down the mountainside. The bonfire roars until late into the night and friends-now-family that gather around a common table are reluctant to leave each other. They linger as the stars fill the Himalayan sky.

breaking bread

R
E
A
D

↳

HEBREWS 12:1-3

CHOOSING JOY IN THE HARD THINGS

REFLECTION

- Jesus had to walk a difficult path on this earth.

- How was He able to overcome? The joy set before Him, the joy of obedience to the Father, the joy of finishing what the Father sent Him to do, the joy of offering salvation to all people, and the joy of bringing rejoicing in Heaven.

- How can we overcome on the difficult road of life? By fixing our eyes on Jesus, looking to Jesus, and remembering all He did for us.

- When we keep our eyes on Jesus, He will give us the grace to endure and to overcome.

REMEMBRANCE

As you break the bread and drink the cup together today...

- Remember the sacrifice of Jesus for you.
- Remember that He walked this difficult road not thinking of himself, but of us.
- Remember Jesus joyfully sacrificed all so that all would be saved.

COMMITMENT

Today I covenant with Christ to offer myself joyfully to fulfill the plan of the Father that all people would be saved. I will not complain or despise the work Jesus has given me to do. I choose to serve with joy.

WEEK 5, DAY 1

An invitation to strategic decisions.

Choosing God, others, and then yourself can be easier stated than lived. Take a moment to write out how your life would look different if you lived your priorities in that order.

To what would you need to say no?

_____

_____

_____

_____

_____

_____

_____

_____

_____

_____

_____

_____

WEEK 5, DAY 2

An invitation to greater character.

When the answer to our passion is "not right now," it can be both hurtful and disillusioning. But, often times, when this happens, God is working on our character.

In what areas do you believe God may be working to improve your character as you wait to pursue your passion?

_____

_____

_____

_____

_____

_____

_____

_____

_____

_____

WEEK 5, DAY 3

An invitation to receive correction.

Has anyone ever pointed out to you an area in which you could improve? What was that area, and how did you receive their advice?

Take a moment to talk to God about your response to correction, and invite Him to help you make changes.

WEEK 5, DAY 4

An invitation to sacrifice.

At this point in this experience, you've shared your stuff and you've opened your life, but have you committed to give your life? There are literally thousands of people groups in India who have yet to hear the gospel. Who will follow Jesus there? Who will make the sacrifice?

Today, write a note to God and tell Him if you're willing. Invite Him to lead you where you should go.

WEEK 5, DAY 5

An invitation to the India table.

Today, the Live Dead India team invites you to come sit at the table in India. If, as you've been going through this experience, you've felt like you would like to be personally involved with the work, we welcome you.

Write us an email and tell us about yourself *(join@thecommontable.us).*

come to the table

week six

living
pilgrimage

This is an invitation to join God's welcome to the world.

God sent Jesus so that we could comprehend the intensity of His desire for relationship with us and fling wide the door of salvation to all the peoples of the world.

When we accept God's invitation in Jesus to a restored relationship with Him, our hearts, too, are enlarged, and we want to become more welcoming. Read Matthew 9:35-38 and Matthew 10 *(The Message version, if available)* in which Jesus taught His disciples the steps involved in learning how to welcome. You've taken these steps over the last five weeks as the Holy Spirit helped you see yourself and others with new, generous eyes. This awareness causes all of us to be overwhelmed. Jesus' answer to our discomfort is, "On your knees and pray for harvest hands."

So, that's the invitation for these five days of pilgrimage: pray. Pray as you read about individuals whose longing for connection with God leads them to make huge sacrifices in time, money, and distance to have a God-encounter. Ask the Holy Spirit to lead you as you pray. Pray alone. Pray with friends. Pray for India, a land of God-seekers, a land of pilgrimage. As you read the stories of our friends Padma, Shahid and Rafida, Sangmu, Shabad and Sain, and Gaurav, our prayer is that your hearts will be gripped with a desire to join us in offering them God's invitation of salvation and restored relationship with Him.

Write us an email and tell us about yourself. There are opportunities to experience India and work alongside one of our teams. Join us **@thecommontable.us**.

JESUS
WALKS
WITH
US

day

haridwar

HINDU PILGRIMAGE

"I must go to the mountains. I must go to Haridwar and the CharDham." Padma is seated on a mora, her thinning waist-length white hair undone, spilling down her back as her granddaughter, Rohini, brushes it. The winter's chill is long gone from her small town in central India. Gul Mohur trees overflow with bright orange blossoms and the summer sun will soon burn its way across the sky.

"Dadi, what are you talking about? You can't go off to the mountains, not by yourself. Papa would never allow it."

"I must visit Har ki Paudi. I want to see Lord Vishnu's footprint and bathe in the water of the Ganga. It's necessary to do Yatra *(pilgrimage)* at least once in this life. I must open the gateways of heaven. I must wash away my sins to obtain Moksha *(salvation)*. I must perform aarti *(evening prayer)* to the goddess Ganga. I must do it this year before your father carries my ashes to the river."

"It's a long time before Papa will carry your ashes, Dadi. Look how strong you are," Rohini laughs.

"You say that because you are young. When your hair is the color of mine you will understand," she replies.

Padma is only one of tens of millions of Hindus who, this year, will make a spiritual pilgrimage to Haridwar, a 2,000-year-old city on the banks of the Ganges River. Haridwar is located in Uttarakhand, a north Indian mountain state that means "the abode of gods" as there is a multitude of ancient temples situated there. Every mountain is named for a Hindu deity, and every stream has spiritual significance. The name Haridwar literally means "gateway to God." It is one of the holiest sites in Hinduism and is the point where the Ganges River, after flowing 250 kilometers from its origin of the Gangotri glacier, descends from the Himalayan Mountains and enters the northern plains of India. Every twelve years, Haridwar is the site of the Kumbha Mela, a Hindu gathering of over 70 million people, once called humanity's largest festival.

Haridwar is also a departure point to the Char Dham pilgrimage that begins in early spring. Thousands of buses overloaded with pilgrims travel to each of the Char Dham temples— Gangotri, Badrinath, Yamunotri, and Kedarnath—and every year, there are buses that never make it to the destination. Hundreds of pilgrims die on the narrow road that rises over 11,000 feet and traverses some of the most dangerous, remote landscape in India. Some pilgrims are able to travel by taxi or private car, or for a small fortune a one-day circuit by helicopter can be arranged. There are also tens of thousands who walk, many for months, many of them old or sick, some carried for miles by family members. Their goal is to have darshan, a spiritual vision, at each of these holy sites of the Hindu religion, and if their karma is good, perhaps they will die while on pilgrimage, guaranteeing a higher reincarnation

in their next life.

Some visitors come out of curiosity to experience the Ganges River by night, illuminated by a myriad of palm-sized clay lamps that float downstream with the current. But the majority have made a long, dangerous, and expensive journey as an act of religious devotion. For them this is a quest with a purpose, the purpose of salvation. Their longing is to have an encounter with God that will guarantee their future.

day two

ajmer

MUSLIM PILGRIMAGE

Shahid is a good Bengali Muslim. He attends Friday Jumu'ah noon prayers at his local mosque where his father-in-law is the imam. Shahid always makes sure to have extra rupees in the pocket of his kurta, so that he can pay the zakat to sick and elderly beggars who gather outside the gate. He has been much more faithful to that practice since his father's death. He tries to observe the other daily prayer times when his schedule permits, but he and his two younger brothers own the largest saree shop in the bazaar and life is busy. The azaan *(call to prayer)* sounds five times a day, and the brothers take turns waiting on customers so each can slip into the back of the shop where they keep their prayer mat. Shahid observes sawm, the fast during the month of Ramadan, and this year the brothers even closed the shop for an hour at sundown to eat the iftar meal together as a family.

Muslims comprise thirteen percent of India's massive 1.3 billion people. Indian Muslims are the world's second largest Muslim population after Indonesia, and they are a fast-growing community in every state of India, fervent in their expressions of faith. Bengali Muslims constitute the world's second-largest Muslim ethnicity *(after the Arab world)* and the largest Muslim community in South Asia.

Shahid and his brother's shop, Kolkata House of Saree, is known for its extensive selection and specializes in clothing for weddings. Although computers and online wholesale companies have expedited ordering, Shahid still prefers to travel to Veranasi to handpick Banarasi sarees. They are among the finest silk sarees in India, embellished with gold and silver brocade or opulent embroidery of zari thread. His own wife, Rafida, wore a red and gold Banarasi saree from his shop on their wedding day five years ago.

Five years is a long time to be married without having a child. Shahid had hoped to provide his father with a grandchild, preferably a grandson to carry on the family name, but his father died six months ago without the fulfillment of that hope. Now his mother and brothers are pressuring him to take a second wife. It's not an easy decision for Shahid, although Rafida, with tears in her eyes, has also broached the topic. Their marriage was an arranged marriage that quickly blossomed

into love, and Shahid longs for a family with Rafida. They have tried everything they know to do: multiple doctor visits and medical tests, special prayers, and amulets. They even attended a Hindu ayurvedic seminar that guaranteed a cure for infertility. His father-in-law, the imam, told Shahid that if he goes on the hajj to Mecca, certainly Allah will hear and answer, but Shahid already borrowed money from everyone he knew to send his father on the hajj before his death.

Shahid has chosen another pilgrimage. He and Rafida are traveling together by train across the breadth of India to the heart of Rajasthan. There in the small town of Ajmer is the Ajmer Sharif Dargah, a shrine to the sufi saint, Moinuddin Chisti. Over 150,000 pilgrims visit the site every day of the year. Akbar, the great mogul king, and his queen used to come here from Agra. Every year they walked all the way to fulfill a vow he made when he prayed for the birth of a son. Shahid and Rafida are hopeful that Allah will answer their pilgrimage by granting them a son.

FIVE YEARS IS A LONG TIME TO BE MARRIED WITHOUT HAVING A CHILD.

day three

dharamsala

BUDDHIST PILGRIMAGE

Sangmu wakes early on this bright Wednesday morning. Her walk to His Holiness' temple will be significantly easier today since the monsoon rains are finally done. Last week she felt like she was in the middle of a rushing river that swept bazaar trash and dirt along with it. Today, the sky is brilliant, and the early sun flashes off the snow peaks that encircle Dharamsala.

Any other day, Sangmu throws on jeans and a T-shirt and leaves her hair loose down her back, but Wednesdays are different. This is the day Tibetan Buddhists pray for long life for the Dalai Lama. She is a fortunate one because she can walk to his temple to pray. Some day she hopes to move to America or Europe, but for now this is her weekly pilgrimage. Sangmu bathes, combs and braids her thick black hair, and wraps herself in the chupa. Her chupa is an oversized, deep blue robe with wide sleeves and a gold-colored blouse underneath. When she marries, she'll also wear the brightly stripped apron, but who knows when that might be. She's quite sure that Dorjee, the college classmate with whom she's in love, will not be her mother's choice for a future son-in-law.

Sangmu walks leisurely down the narrow street toward His Holiness' temple. On the left, the shops, grocery stores, and restaurants advertise their wares with shouting shopkeepers and tantalizing aromas. On the right, homespun shops sell handicrafts and religious items: prayer beads, incense holders, and singing brass bowls. Further down the road, men sell the beautiful white khatas that Tibetans give as gifts after having them blessed at the temple. The white cloths hold deep significance for Buddhists: when the Dalai Lama visits the town, crowds line the road and hold out khatas to be blessed by him.

Every day thousands of visitors throng to the temple that was built around the trees that grow within it. The courtyard holds new trees that have been planted over the years. Someday they will provide shade to the monks who practice debates on the lawn. Tourists often find amusement as they watch the monks call and respond to one another, clapping to accent their points and laughing when a fellow makes a mistake. Scores of people—Indian, Tibetan, and Western—flock upstairs to circle the upper floor which houses the Golden Buddha, as well as the secondary chamber holding

other protective deities of the Tibetan people.

Sangmu adds her shoes to the hundreds left at the doorway. She enters the prayer room with the crowd and prostrates herself before the golden statue. She always feels a deep sense of history and awe when she thinks about the millions of times this same act has been performed on this same spot. She passes the artwork on the walls and the piles of offerings in the forms of food and cash. She sees the collection of holy books written in their original Sanskrit, rescued from Tibet and brought here for safekeeping. Sangmu's favorite bench is just beside the room filled with hundreds of butter lamps that the local monks and nuns always keep lit. Sangmu's voice joins the thousands of other voices chanting mantras. She moves around the back of the temple and prayerfully spins the golden prayer wheels. She is certain that her acts of worship and prayer will result in long life for His Holiness, the Dalai Lama.

DAY FOUR

AMRITSA

SIKH PILGRIMAGE

Shabad Singh leans forward. His dark eyes are alight with spiritual intensity. He is always emotional when he speaks about his visit to the Sri Harmandir Sahib *(Golden Temple)* in Amritsar, Punjab. He would never call the visit a pilgrimage since his religion condemns blind rituals. He is a Sikh, a disciple of God who follows the writings and teachings of the Ten Sikh Gurus. He is also a Khalsa, initiated into the way of life in the amrit pahul *(nectar ceremony)*. He accepts the behavioral code, Rahit, which includes no tobacco, no alcohol, and no halal meat. Shabad follows the dress code of Sikhism as well, defined by the panj kakar *(Five K's)*: Kesh, *(uncut hair)*, Kangha *(wooden comb for the hair)*, Kara *(iron bracelet)*, Kachera *(undergarment)*, and Kirpan *(iron dagger large enough for self-defense)*.

When Shabad, whose name means "light of the holy word," was 35, he traveled with his wife Sain to the Golden Temple. It is considered the holiest gurdwara of Sikhism. He went to have darshan, a spiritual vision, and was overwhelmed when he saw the beautiful golden building surrounded by the waters of the Sarovar. The decorative gilding and exquisite marble ceiling with inlaid precious stones create a work of art. He was proud to know that his religious community still stands after the persecution it experienced. Here he felt the sacrifices of his ancestors who had given their lives in defense of their faith—some sawed in half, another pulled apart by horses, and others beheaded. Shabad has heard their stories from childhood but being in the holy place made their lives and deaths more precious to him.

Shabad and Sain looked forward to the meal they would enjoy at the langar *(kitchen)*. The Sri Harmandir Sahib is home to the world's largest kitchen; it serves food to all visitors regardless of faith, religion, or background. Today, over 100,000 people will enjoy free vegetarian meals, served to ensure that all people, even those with dietary restrictions, can eat together as equals. This tradition expresses the Sikh ethic of sharing, community, inclusiveness, and oneness of all people.

Shabad and Sain started across the long causeway over the lake with thousands of others who came for darshan. Sain leaned on her husband's arm, determined they would experience this together. Quiet and gentle, Sain lived with a painful secret. Her feet were covered with open sores, her soles cracked and bleeding. It was agonizing to walk. She always wore socks to cover and protect her feet. Pilgrims removed their shoes at the entrance, taking advantage of the storing system provided by the gurdwara administration. Sain removed her shoes but not her socks. A guard at the door informed Shabad that they would only be allowed to enter if Sain's socks were removed. In respect for this place, all feet must be bare. Shabad explained their dilemma but the guard had his orders. Sain took off her socks and washed her feet along with the others who were preparing to enter and pray. It was hours later, after they experienced the beauty of the gurdwara, prayed, and ate lunch that Shabad and Sain realized what happened. Sain's feet were healed. They always believed that God was everywhere, but it was here that they experienced God.

"HE WHO SEARCHES FOR DIVINE REALITY WITH ALL HIS HEART AND SOUL AND FINDS IT, BECOMES AWARE THAT, BEFORE HE BEGAN TO SEEK GOD, GOD WAS SEEKING HIM, IN ORDER TO DRAW HIM INTO THE JOY OF FELLOWSHIP WITH HIM, INTO THE PEACE OF HIS PRESENCE."

- Sadhu Sundar Singh

SELF

SECULAR PILGRIMAGE

Hurtling across Rajasthan-Jaipur to Delhi on an A/C Double Decker train, I paid $5 for this three and a half hour journey. My last train trip was with Dale as we returned from Shantiniketan with our young rooftop friends.

This is a very different landscape from West Bengal. It's dry and barely green with stubby hills and timeworn stone outposts. There are no abundant rice fields or yellow-flowered mustard crops. No glistening rivers with fish jumping. It's barely 7 a.m., and the sun is already on high. The temperature will reach 115 degrees today. Everything withers in such heat. Even weeds hide. This landscape makes me think about Jesus' story of the sower and the seed: hard paths, rocks, burning sun, weeds, and bird thieves. I think about what it takes to plant a seed so deep it can take root and grow and reproduce. I think about young Indians in the middle of an ancient culture. India is like an archeological dig with shopping malls, cappuccino, and blue jeans on the surface but 4,000 years of history below, and every layer of history informs the lives of those who live on the surface today.

Jesus told such engaging stories which are not out of place in India. Even superimposed on this land, they don't appear imposed at all. They are stories and land that go together.

like tea and biscuits on an Indian afternoon. Many of Jesus' stories are common table stories: an insistent midnight neighbor; an untimely guest that needs a meal in the middle of the night; a wedding at which Jesus multiplies wine; another wedding for which everyone receives a hand-delivered invitation; the runaway son eating pig feed before returning home to a banquet; multiple mealtimes sitting, eating, and sharing with sinners and outsiders; and finally a gathering of friends to participate in an ancient, God-ordained meal, a meal with a meaning and a message on the eve of a religious pilgrimage. In that moment, as He often did, Jesus took the historic and made it contemporary, took the symbolic and made it incarnate.

India is the youngest nation in the world. The median age is 27.6, which means half the people are younger and half are older than this age. Over 65 percent of the country is under 30. As I think about the Jesus stories and how relevant they are to this young country, a young man drops into seat 21B, right next to me on the train: jeans, T-shirt, iPod, and earphones with music blaring. I think he's listening to Arcade Fire. He glances at me and apologizes for the loud music.

"Actually, I like your music. I just worry about your eardrums," I respond.

He laughs. "My mother says the same thing."

"I guess mothers were created to worry." We both laugh.

"I'm Gaurav," he introduces himself.

"And I'm Beth. Your mom told me to keep an eye on you." At that he laughs out loud.

The attendant delivers trays to each seat. He sets down a cup of chai, milky-sweet, with two cookies and a vegetable samosa served with ketchup and spicy achar on the side. Eating together, Gaurav and I begin to talk. Our conversation is lively. It covers a global landscape: music, movies, books, Facebook, politicians old and new, infrastructure, roads, railways, Internet connections, job opportunities, American universities, money, extreme poverty, family expectations, religious observances, and smart young Indians. I tell him that Dale used to say, "America is the past and India is the future, and we'd better get used to it." He's surprised but pleased to hear that declaration from me.

I ask Gaurav what he lives for, if he's ever felt the need to go on a religious pilgrimage. He's not reticent to tell me. He lives for a good education and the income to be earned from his chosen profession. He wants to make a lot of money and have a lot of fun along the way. No, he's not religious and has never been on a pilgrimage. He doesn't believe in any gods, but he honors his parents, grandparents, and great grandparents, and their beliefs and way of life.

"What do you think are India's biggest problems?" I ask him. He begins to list the enormity of things that must be overcome to usher in a promising future—population growth, illiteracy, and corruption. I feel the weight that he feels, the seeming impossibilities.

Then he asks me, "What do you think is the biggest problem for young Indians?"

I pause. This is where my story, Gaurav's story, and Jesus' story meet on a train bound for Delhi. "Please forgive me if I'm direct."

"Of course, of course," he says. "Mothers have the right to be direct."

"Selfishness," I say, "and it's not just a young Indian problem. The disease, like the cure, is ancient and global."

"IF WE FIND OURSELVES WITH A DESIRE THAT NOTHING IN THIS WORLD CAN SATISFY, THE MOST PROBABLE EXPLANATION IS THAT WE WERE MADE FOR ANOTHER WORLD."

- C.S. Lewis

breaking
bread

R
E
A
D

↳

1 PETER 2:11–12

HEART OF A
PILGRIM

REFLECTION

- In the world there are always things trying to pull us away from the pure pursuit of Christ. What is it that keeps you from living wholeheartedly for Jesus *(money, relationships, ambition, dreams, etc.)*?

- Remembering that this world is not our home and that we are just passing through is essential to living our lives for the glory of God. It not only leads to a life that is pure but to others seeing Christ in us.

- The purpose of life is to bring glory to God, that everyone we meet would see Christ in us.

REMEMBRANCE

As you break the bread and drink the cup together today...

- Remember that your home is not of this world. You were purchased with the blood of Jesus, and you are a citizen of the Kingdom of Heaven.

- Remember that we are the body of Christ. We are not alone in this journey. Thank you, Lord, we are not on this pilgrimage alone.

- Remember the purpose of this pilgrimage is to make Jesus famous in all the earth. We are here for a purpose—until everyone knows that Jesus is Lord.

COMMITMENT

I covenant today to hold loosely to the things of this world, to living my life for the Kingdom of Heaven, not to build my kingdom on earth. I covenant that all the days of my pilgrimage of earth will be dedicated to making Jesus known to all I meet, wherever I am: at my school, work, neighborhood, and wherever You will send me.

A FULFILLED PILGRIMAGE

Jesus followers are also on pilgrimage. The difference for us is that we experience the goal and the fulfillment of our pilgrimage every day. Jesus walks with us. His face and fame are ever before us. His Spirit indwells us. His final glory is our goal.

We see ourselves as guests in this world. We accepted the invitation to a life full of adventure as we follow Jesus. We are not running away. Instead, we are choosing to enter more deeply into life and the world around us. We are leaving behind distractions and pettiness to seek God in all things and to dedicate ourselves to fully do His will, and we are willing to make the necessary decisions that some might not understand.

These last six weeks, we began to prove our commitment by setting aside time and space for this quest. We accepted Jesus' invitation week by week as we came to a common table to remember and commit. We are joyful in the convergence of West and East as family called to a common dream: the gospel lived and proclaimed to the ends of the earth. We embraced loss as gain, and we will endure any inconvenience, suffer any sacrifice, and lay down our very lives to make Jesus famous. We are ready to extend the common table, to invite strangers to become family. We are now ready to be God's welcome to the world.

"KEEP OPEN HOUSE; BE GENEROUS WITH YOUR LIVES. BY OPENING UP TO OTHERS YOU'LL PROMPT PEOPLE TO OPEN UP WITH GOD, THIS GENEROUS FATHER IN HEAVEN."

Matthew 5:15-16

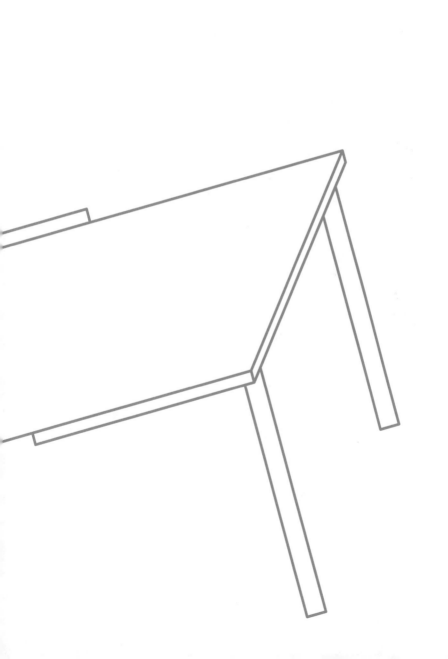

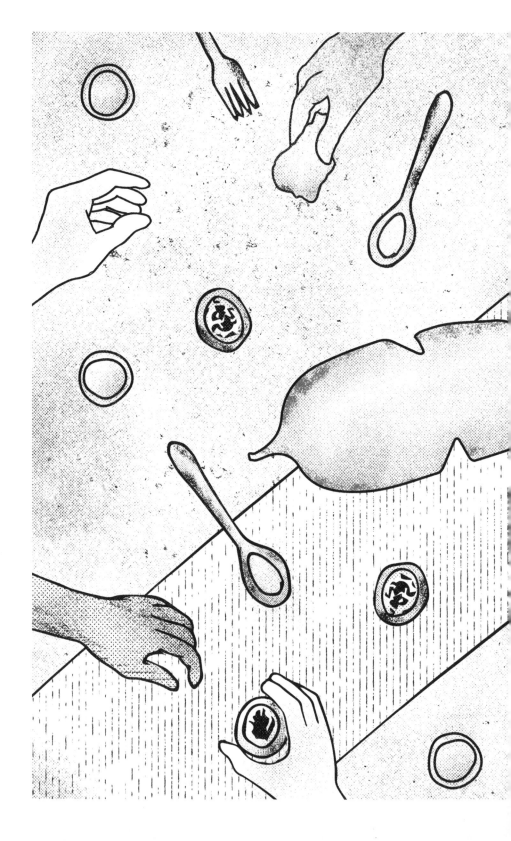